FRANCIS PIEPER

Conversion and Election

First published by Just and Sinner 2020

Copyright © 2020 by Francis Pieper

All rights reserved. No part of this publication may be reproduced, stored or transmitted in any form or by any means, electronic, mechanical, photocopying, recording, scanning, or otherwise without written permission from the publisher. It is illegal to copy this book, post it to a website, or distribute it by any other means without permission.

Though the original text is in the public domain, regarding this updated edition, no part shall be copied or distributed without permission. Inquiries may be sent to contact@justandsinner.org

Just and Sinner

Ithaca, NY 14850

www.jspublishing.org

First edition

ISBN: 978-1-952295-06-5

This book was professionally typeset on Reedsy. Find out more at reedsy.com

Contents

Prefatory Remarks	iv
Norwegian Articles of Agreement	1
Two Conceptions of Election	5
The Fundamental Difference	14
An Injustice Done the Norwegian Synod	20
Madison Theses and the Rejection of Synergism	25
Conversion by Means of "New Powers Imparted by Grace"	31
The Point of Difference Stated by the Formula	36
Assent of All Christians to the Presentation	41
Position of the Old Dogmaticians	47
Preparation for Conversion	90
The Possibility of Conversion	104
Two Concepts of Calling	109
Fellowship of Faith and Church	114
Which Side Changed Its Position?	119
A Few Opinions that Have Been Expressed	129

Prefatory Remarks

Prefatory Remarks.[1]

During the last forty years there has been a public discussion within the Lutheran Church of America of the doctrine of election and, in connection therewith, of the doctrine of conversion. The controversy concerning these doctrines was of such seriousness that it brought about divisions and new alliances. Also the oldest Norwegian church-society in America, the Norwegian Synod, was not only drawn into the controversy, but also suffered grievous damage in consequence of a division which occurred among its constituents. Recently efforts of greater magnitude than at previous times have been made to reunite the Norwegian Lutherans. Moreover, these efforts have produced palpable results. Articles of Agreement have been drawn up by a joint committee and have been almost unanimously adopted by the respective synods. These events, however, have caused a renewal of the public discussion, in the press of the Church, of the doctrines of election and conversion.

We need not regret this. The subject about which everything turns in the last analysis is the subject *De servo arbitrio* and *De libero arbitrio*, that is, the question whether in matters spiritual the natural will of man is of no moment, or whether it can accomplish something. This subject will retain a decisive importance for the Church until the end of days. Luther treated this subject not only at Heidelberg in 1518, and over and against Erasmus in 1525, but to the end of his life. In comparison with the subject of free will, he calls all other controversies which he had with the Romanists "puerile affairs" and "remote matters." He addresses Erasmus, who ascribed to man a *facultas se*

---

[1] Translation by Prof. W. H. T. Dau, in Theological Quarterly, 1913, pp. 131 sqq.

applicandi ad gratiam, a good conduct in spiritual matters, thus:

This is what I commend and praise in you, *viz.*, that before all the rest you alone have attacked the real matter, that is, the central issue, and have not wearied me with those remote matters (*alienis illis causis*) concerning the papacy, purgatory, indulgences, and such matters, which are puerilities (*nugae*) rather than issues. With such matters nearly all others have hitherto vainly pursued me. You are the only person that has seen the real point in controversy, and have taken me by the throat (*cardinem rerum vidisti et ipsium jugulim petisti*). For this I thank you with all my heart; for I delight to be occupied with this subject, as far as my time and leisure will permit.[2]

A discussion of this subject is necessary also in our times. It is not easy for theologians to keep their balance in this question. It is different with Christians. On the basis of Scripture Christians simply believe: A person who is converted and saved is converted and saved by the grace of God alone; if a person remains unconverted and is lost, the blame rests on himself. This fact is expressed in theological parlance thus: On the basis of Scripture, Christians believe the doctrine of *sola gratia* as well as that of *universalis gratia*. However, we meet with a different state of affairs among theologians. Theologians imagine that they are forced to deny or to "limit"—thus they usually put it euphemistically—either the one doctrine or the other. Shedd, with the utmost seriousness, divides all Christians on earth into two classes of people: such as deny the doctrine of *sola gratia,* and such as deny the doctrine of *universalis gratia*.[3] From the view-point of the theologian he denies to the Lutheran Church, which confesses and maintains both doctrines, especially in the 11th Article of the Form of Concord, and which places its veto, in the very premises, on every effort to mediate between these two doctrines, also on the so-called theological effort, calling such efforts "presumption," the right to exist. Shedd and other Reformed theologians of recent times designate the

---

[2] Opp. v. a. VII, 367, St. Louis Ed. XVIII, 1967.

[3] Dogmatic Theology, I, 448. According to Shedd there are only "two great systems of theology which divide evangelical Christendom, Calvinism, and Arminianism."

position occupied by the Form of Concord "untenable ground."[4] Luthardt shares this opinion.[5] The difference between Shedd and Luthardt is only this, that, of the two factors which come under consideration at this point, the former cancels or "limits" *universalis gratia*, the latter, *sola gratia*. The position which is in accordance with Scripture, and, hence, is the only correct one from the theological view-point, *viz.,* the position which maintains both *sola gratia* and *universalis gratia*, without diminishing the force of either, has been expressed, as far as we can see, only three times in public documents issued by churches, and recorded in the history of the Christian Church: in the decrees of the Synod of Orange in 529, in the 11th Article of the Form of Concord, in 1580, and in the 13 Theses of the Missouri Synod, in 1881.

In participating, by means of this publication, in discussion of the Norwegian Articles of Agreement, and of the criticism to which they have been subjected, our aim is to aid, on our part, toward the recognition and maintenance of the doctrinal position of the Form of Concord as the only one which is in accordance with Scripture and correct from the theological point of view. Our wish and our prayer to God is, that the Norwegian Lutherans of America in their union, which is most desirable, would place themselves upon a platform which fully corresponds to the glorious confession of the Lutheran Church in the 11th Article. When they have done this, all other Lutherans of America, whether they speak German, English, or any other tongue, should follow the example of Norwegian Lutherans.

If circumstances had been different, we should have preferred to treat the glorious confessional position of the Lutheran Church in the Article of Election once more in the same manner as was done at the intersynodical conference at Watertown, Wis., in 1904. On that occasion we presented the controverted doctrine without quotations from controversial writings which had appeared in America. This was done in order to avoid, as far as possible, the arousing of party feeling. This method is not feasible as matters are at present. The Norwegian Articles of Agreement have been given to the

---

[4] See also Hodge, Systematic Theology, II, 325.

[5] Die Lehre vom freien Willen, p. 276.

public, and have been publicly praised as well as censured in the periodicals of the Church. In these public discussions there is still special mention made of us, the so-called Missourians. On the one hand, the Norwegian theses are being praised for the reason that the doctrinal position of the Missouri Synod is being combated by them. On the other hand, the same theses are being censured, for the reason that their contents are essentially Missourian. Moreover, individual persons in our circles are being specially referred to in these discussions, *vis.*, Walther before others, but also members of the present St. Louis Faculty. Quite a number of particular questions are being treated more or less exhaustively, for instance, the question, whether there are two forms of presenting the doctrine of election, which ultimately merge into one doctrine, as far as their contents are concerned. Since the Articles of Agreement mention the names of Gerhard, Scriver, and Pontoppidan, a new discussion has arisen regarding the position maintained by ourselves and our opponents as regards the doctrine of the later Lutheran dogmaticians. Since the doctrine of election cannot be treated without reference to the doctrine of conversion, the question has again been called up for debate, whether a person's conversion is dependent upon the grace of God alone or also upon the person's proper conduct; again, what is the meaning of the "call," and whether it is admissible to speak of "the possibility of being converted," and of "acts preparatory to conversion." Lastly, also this delicate question has been raised, "Which side has changed its position?" Our purpose is to throw some light on all these question, however, solely to the end of aiding in bringing about a union on the glorious platform of our Lutheran Confessions.

1

Norwegian Articles of Agreement

I. The Norwegian Articles of Agreement

The Norwegian Articles of Agreement, also called the Madison Agreement, having been adopted at Madison, Wis., read as follows:

"1. The Synod and United Church Committees on Union acknowledge unanimously and without reservation the doctrine of Predestination which is stated in the Eleventh Article of the Formula of Concord (the so-called 'first form of the doctrine') and in Pontoppidan's Explanation (*Sanshed til Gudfrygtighed*), Question 548 (the so-called 'second form of the doctrine').

"2. Whereas the conferring church bodies acknowledge that Art. XI of the Formula of Concord presents the pure and correct doctrine of God's Word and the Lutheran Church regarding the election of the children of God to salvation, it is deemed unnecessary to church union to construct new and more extensive theses concerning this article of faith.

"3. But since, in regard to the doctrine of Election, it is well known that two forms of the doctrine have been used, both of which have been recognized as correct in the Lutheran Church, *viz.*, that some, with the Formula of Concord, make the doctrine of Election to comprise the entire salvation of the elect from the calling to the glorification,—cf.; Thorough Explanation,' Article XI,

§§ 10—12,—and teach an election 'to salvation through sanctification by the Spirit and faith in the truth,' while others, like Pontoppidan, in consonance with John Gerhard, Scriver, and other acknowledged doctrinal fathers, define Election specifically as the decree of final glorification, with the Spirit's work of faith and perseverance as its necessary postulate, and teach that 'God has ordained to eternal life all those who from eternity He foresaw would accept the proffered grace, believe in Christ, and remain steadfast in this faith unto the end'; and since neither of those two forms of doctrine, presented in this wise, contradicts any doctrine revealed in the Word of God, but lets the order of salvation, as otherwise presented in God's Word and the Confession of the Church, remain entirely intact and fully acknowledged,—we find, that this fact ought not to be divisive of church unity, nor ought it disrupt that unity of Spirit in the bond of peace which God wills should obtain between us.

"4. Since, however, during the doctrinal controversy among us, words and expressions have been used—rightly or wrongly attributed to one party or the other—which seemed to the other side a denial of the Confession of the Church, or to lead to such denial, we have agreed to reject all erroneous doctrines which seek to explain away the mystery of Election (Formula of Concord, Art. XI, §§39-44) either in a synergistic manner or in a Calvinizing way; in other words, we reject every doctrine which either, on the one hand, would rob God of His honor as the only Savior, or, on the other, would weaken man's sense of responsibility in respect of the acceptance or rejection of God's grace.

"5. On the other hand, we reject:

"a) The doctrine, that God's mercy and the most holt merits of Christ are not the sole reason for our election, but that there is also in ourselves a reason for such election, for the sake of which God has ordained us to eternal life.

"b) The doctrine, that in election God has been determined by, or has taken into account, or has been actuated by, man's good conduct, or by anything which man is or may do or omit to do, 'as of himself or by his own natural powers.'

"c) The doctrine, that the faith in Christ which is indissolubly connected with election is wholly or in part a product of, or dependent upon, man's own choosing, power, or ability.

"d) Or, that this faith is the result of a power and ability imparted to man by the call of grace, and therefore now dwelling in, and belonging to, the unregenerate man, to decide himself for grace.

"6. On the other hand, we reject:

"a) The doctrine, that in election God acts arbitrarily and without motive, and picks out and counts a certain arbitrary number of indiscriminate individuals, and ordains these to conversion and salvation, while passing by all the others.

"b) The doctrine, that there are two different kinds of will regarding salvation in God, one revealed in the Scriptures in the general order of salvation, and another, differing from this, and unknown to us, which relates only to the elect, and imparts a deeper love, a more effective call from God, and a larger measure of grace than are brought to him who remains in unbelief and condemnation.

"c) The doctrine, that when the resistance which God in conversion removes from those whom He saves is not taken away in others, who finally are lost, this different result finds its cause in God and in a differing will of salvation in His act of election.

"d) The doctrine, that a believer can and ought to have an absolute assurance of his election and salvation, instead of an assurance of faith, built upon the promise of God, and joined with fear and trembling by the possibility of falling from grace, which, however, by the mercy of God he believes will not become a reality in his case.

"e) In summary, all views and doctrines regarding Election which directly or indirectly come into conflict with the order of salvation, and do not give to all a full and, therefore, equally great opportunity of salvation, or which in any manner would invalidate that word of God which declares that; God will have all men to be saved and come unto the knowledge of the truth'—in which gracious and merciful will of God all election to eternal life has its origin.

"On the basis of the above Agreement the Committees on Union memorialize their respective church-bodies to adopt the following "Resolution.

"Whereas, our Confessions determine that 'to the true unity of the Church it is sufficient that there be agreement in the doctrine of the Gospel and in the administration of the Sacrament;' and

"Whereas, our former committees, by the grace of God, have attained unity in the doctrines concerning the Calling, Conversion, and in general, the Order of Salvation, and we all confess as our sincere faith that we are saved by grace alone, without any cooperation on our part; and

"Whereas, the negotiations of our new committees have led to a satisfactory agreement concerning the doctrine of Election, and to an unreserved and unanimous acknowledgement of the doctrine of Election which is presented in the Formula of Concord, 'Thorough Explanation,' Art. XI, and in Pontoppidan's *Sandhed til Gudfrygtighed*, Question 548,—now, therefore,

"*Be it resolved*, That we declare hereby that the essential unity concerning these doctrines which now is attained is sufficient to church union.

"May Almighty God, the Father of our Lord Jesus Christ, grant us the grace of His Holy Spirit, that we all may be one in Him and ever remain steadfast in such Christian and God-pleasing union! Amen."

The position of the Norwegian Synod's committee was stated as follows at the various district conventions of 1912 which ratified the committee's report:

Question 1: "Is there anything in paragraph one (§1) which is essentially different from paragraph three (§3) of the 'Agreement'?" — *Answer*: "No."

Question 2: "If we accept paragraph one (§1), do we thereby accept the so-called second form of the doctrine?" — *Answer*: "In the first paragraph no form is accepted, but the doctrine contained in two forms. The Norwegian Synod's committee accepts without reservation the first form of the doctrine as that of Scripture and the Confession, but can nevertheless recognize as brethren those who hold the second form as seen in the light of the subsequent paragraphs of the 'Agreement.'"

2

Two Conceptions of Election

II. The Two Conceptions of the Election of Grace.

How have the Norwegian theses been received? Unfortunately, in most instances where judgement has been passed on them, the censors have promptly dragged the Missouri Synod into the discussion by raising the question: "What is the attitude which these theses assume toward Missouri?" According as this question has been answered, there has been uttered irrelevant praise or censure. The theses have been accorded irrelevant praise—praise from the Iowa Synod's point of view—in the Iowa *Kirchenblatt*, which declares that by the Norwegian theses, the Missourian conception of Election has been given a deadly blow. Unquestionably the purport of this remark of the *Kirchenblatt* is, that the "Missourian" conception of Election is combated, if not rejected, in the Norwegian theses. Is this a correct representation of the state of affairs? Hardly.

The Norwegian Agreement presents *two* conceptions of the doctrine of Election, which are carefully distinguished and clearly delimited the one from the other. According to the first conception, Election is "a choosing unto salvation through sanctification of the Spirit and belief of the truth." Accordingly, "The doctrine of Election comprises the entire salvation of the elect, from the calling to glorification." According to the second conception, God "has ordained to eternal life all those who from eternity He foresaw would accept the proffered grace, believe in Christ, and remain steadfast to the end." According to this second conception, Election does not include the *entire* salvation of the elect from their call to their glorification, but refers only to the ultimate result, "the final glorification," and faith wrought by the Holy Spirit does not enter into the eternal election as a component part, but is a "necessary antecedent" of election. The first conception is generally known as the "Missourian," the second conception, with its characteristic "election in view of faith," has been declined by Missouri. Iowa has never ceased to find fault with us for our refusal to accept this second conception.

Now, what is the attitude of the Norwegian theses toward the first conception of Election? It is acknowledged in plain terms, in Theses 2 and 3, that the first conception—the "Missourian"—is the conception of the Scriptures and the Lutheran Confessions. As regards the second conception, the one characterized by the formula "in view of faith," according to which faith is a necessary antecedent of election, it is not claimed at all that this conception is taught in the Scriptures and the Lutheran Confessions. On the contrary, it is expressly stated that this conception is peculiar to later Lutheran theologians, such as Pontoppidan, Gerhard, Scriver, and others, that it gained entrance into the Church upon the authority of these great men, and that this conception, when understood and explained so as to exclude every synergistic notion, leaves the doctrine of the way of salvation intact. Hence the Norwegian theses do not reject, but declare, the Missourian doctrine of Election to be the doctrine *of Scripture and of the Lutheran Confessions*.

We are aware of the following objection at this point: "If your Missourian conception of Election is expressly recognized in the Agreement as the conception of Scripture and the Lutheran Confessions, then, why are you not entirely satisfied with the theses?" The reason why we are not quite satisfied, and why we beg leave to offer a suggestion, is stated in the Agreement itself. It is this: the second conception, which regards election as having taken place "in view of faith," is not the conception of Scripture and the Lutheran Confessions, but of later theologians. Now, we are convinced that anything not taught by the Scriptures nor the Lutheran Confessions should not be embodied in a platform in which Lutheran church bodies purpose to declare their unity in the faith. Moreover, the Norwegian bodies primarily concerned in this union movement agree with us in the *principle* that articles of faith are established only by Holy Writ, not by the authority of theologians. Even the Lutheran Confessions, to be sure, are accepted by all of us for this sole reason, because (*quia*) they profess nothing beside the Scriptures, but *only* the Scriptures. For this reason we believe that the Norwegian church bodies will concur with us in declaring that the second conception, which is not found in Scripture, and, for this reason, is not professed in the Lutheran Confessions, ought to be stricken from their articles of church union. This is our well-meant suggestion. When the Iowa *kirchenblatt*, some months ago, maintained that "Missouri" desired no union of the Lutheran synods in America on the basis of the Lutheran Confessions, and again, when the same journal recently reiterated the charge that Missouri is an enemy of "all true union," such remarks must be classed with the aforesaid irrelevant utterances, and they are best explained as arising from the party-spirit. We "Missourians" would like to do our share towards bringing about among the Lutheran church bodies of America a union worthy of the Church of the Reformation, that is to say, a union on the basis of the Scriptures and the Confessions, because the Confessions state only the doctrine of the Scriptures and no human opinions.

   A question here arises which is apt to dim our vision of the exclusive right which must be accorded the teaching of the Scriptures and the Confessions. It is this: What shall be our attitude toward those teachers, otherwise highly esteemed by us, who cling to the "in-view-of-faith: formula; more especially, how shall we regard those teachers who in the last analysis *explain* this formula so as to give it a meaning different from its native sense? As, when we hear it stated: "We accept the term 'in view of faith' *as a description of the elect in the present life*. What we wish to express by means of this phrase is merely this, that those are the elect who are in this life believers and depart this life in the faith." Now, this explanation, or interpretation, of the "second form: of the doctrine of Election has been given in express terms by theologians of the Norwegian Synod. Again, it has been aid: By using the formula "in view of faith," we desire to express the fact that the sanctification of the Spirit and faith in Christ form a component part of the eternal election, and are not, as the Calvinists teach, merely means of carrying into execution an election already brought about without the sanctification of the Spirit and faith in Christ. Thus explained and interpreted the second form, as regards the *matter* taught, is indeed no longer placed in contradiction to the first. However, in that case everybody will grant that we must apply the rule: *Tene mentem corrige linguam*, that is, Keep your correct thought, but drop your faulty expression. Accordingly, Walther advised as early as 1872:

We believe that the safest way to avoid every kind of misunderstanding is to forbear using the new terminology of the seventeenth-century theologians, and to return to the simplicity of the Formula of Concord, which does not attempt to solve the mystery.[6]

In the interest of reaching an understanding regarding the matter involved, this point deserves to be examined more closely. It is indeed correct doctrine that the elect are, not those who are unbelievers in this life, but those who believe and remain steadfast in faith. This is what the *Scriptures* teach. In John 10, 27 Christ describes His elect according to their temporal aspect on earth thus: "My sheep hear my voice; I know them, and they follow me." V. 5: "A stranger will they not follow, but will flee from him; for they know not the voice of strangers." According to Matt. 22, the elect, as distinguished from those who are merely called, are those who obey the call to the wedding and have on the wedding garment. The same truth is expressed in our Lutheran Confessions:

For this reason the elect are *described* thus: 'My sheep hear my voice; and I know them, and they follow me; and I give them eternal life.' (John 10:29 sq.) And (Eph. 1:11, 13): Who according to the purpose are predestined to an inheritance, hear the Gospel, believe in Christ, pray and give thanks, are sanctified in love, have hope, patience, and comfort under the cross. (Rom.

---

[6] L.&W., 1872, p. 140. We shall quote later Walther's opinion on those who make *intuitu fidei* a cloak of synergism.

8.)[7]

But this correct doctrine does *not* find *expression* in the second conception of Election. The formula, "Election in view of steadfast faith," rather conveys the thought that faith, faith persevering unto the end of life, is an *antecedent* of election; in other words, a person must have received faith, and remained steadfast therein to the end, before God could elect him. Again, it is indeed correct to say that faith constitutes a component part of eternal election itself, and is not given its proper place when it is made a mere afterthought, belonging not to the elective act in eternity, but only to its execution in time. Such a view of the relation of faith to election makes election to be *absolute*, that is to say, it declares election to have taken place, not through sanctification of the Spirit and belief of the truth, but without these. It is *Scripture* that teaches us the proper place of faith in election. 2 Thess. 2:13 describes how election took place in eternity; v. 14, how it is executed in time. According to v. 13, God has chosen men from eternity unto salvation "in the sanctification of the Spirit and belief of the truth." By these words the *mode* of the eternal election is set forth. St. Paul, in this passage, invites the Thessalonians not only to a view of the *fact* that God ordained them from eternity unto salvation, ὅτι εἵλατο ὑμᾶς ὁ θεὸς ἀπαρχὴν εἰς σωτηρίαν, but immediately subjoins a definite statement as regards the *manner* in which this act was performed in eternity, *viz.*, in the sanctification of the Spirit and belief of the truth, ἐν ἁγιασμῷ πνεύματος καὶ πίστει ἀληθείας. This ἐν denotes the accompanying circumstance, the manner how, or the means by which, something is done. As, for instance, in Acts 17:31: God will judge the earth ἐν δικαιοσύνῃ ἐν ἀνδρὶ ᾧ ὥρισεν, "*in* righteousness *by* that man," etc. So frequently. Not only does the phrase, ἐν ἁγιασμῷ πνεύματος καὶ πίστει ἀληθείας, as well as the statement: εἵλατο ὑμᾶς ὁ θεὸς ἀπαρχὴν εἰς σωτηρίαν, belong into *eternity*, but it also belongs into the one eternal *act* of electing. The thought that is here plainly stated is as follows: God has chosen you Christians at Thessalonica from eternity unto salvation; the choosing hand of God took hold of you from everlasting, but not *absolutely* (Latin, *nude*), *merely by His omnipotent hand*, but

---

[7] Mueller, p. 710, §30. Jacobs (People's Edition), p. 655.

through the sanctification of the Spirit and the belief of the truth, that is to say, through the instrument of the Gospel and by the bestowal of faith. Thus, according to the Scriptures, the sanctification of the Spirit, the operation of God through the Gospel, and the conferring of faith belong into the act of the eternal election as such, and not only into its *execution* in time. This very thought is deemed of such importance by our Confession that it makes clear from the outset[8] that eternal election must not be regarded *nude*, absolutely, as though it comprised in itself nothing further, or nothing more belonged thereto, than that God would say thus: This one shall be saved, that one shall be damned, but that the entire doctrine concerning the ordination of God pertaining to our redemption, call, righteousness, and salvation *should be taken together, simul mente complectamur*. For, as God has elected us ἐν Χριστῷ, so also , ἐν ἁγιασμῷ πνεύματος καὶ πίστει ἀληθείας. In other words: Even as Christ belongs into the eternal act of electing as its *basis*, so the Gospel and faith likewise as its *means*. Even as the elect are not taken *nude*, "without means," out of the world into the kingdom of God on earth, but are "by the hearing of His holy divine Word, as with a net...delivered from the jaws of the devil,"[9] even so—in like manner—the eternal act of election was performed.

This point is of decisive importance in teaching Election. If we failed to take *into* Election the net of the Gospel and faith, but imagine election as performed *nude*,—*extra Christum* and *extra evangelium et fidem*,—we should, at the very outset, mutilate the doctrine of Election to such an extent that the damage could not be repaired. Election, in that case, could not but appear "terrible" to us. We should, in that case, be hopelessly committed to the false, Calvinistic conception of an absolute election. And as to the practical use of the doctrine of Election, we could not be directed to seek and fund out eternal election *in the Gospel* as the entire Eleventh Article of the Formula of Concord urges us to do. But if the eternal election was *enacted*, not *nude*, but by means of the Gospel and by the conferring of faith, then our eternal election is also *revealed* to us in time, in each and every instance, by means of

---

[8] Mueller, p. 706, §§ 9. 13. 14. Jacobs, p. 651 f.

[9] Mueller, p. 720, § 76. Jacobs, p. 662.

the Gospel and by our faith in the same. We need only *believe the Gospel* in order to recognize our election and be assured of it. As Luther never ceases to admonish the believer: Make the Gospel your concern, and you will not fail to discover your election.[10] Scruples regarding a person's eternal election can arise only at such times as, and in the event that, *he lets go of the Gospel and of faith*. Such is the overshadowing importance of the truth that the Gospel and faith belong into the *act* of eternal election itself, and not merely into its execution. Dr. Walther says:

Our doctrine is this: Even as God in time saves us *by faith*, even so He from eternity decreed to save the elect *by faith*; and this is what is meant by the decree of election in the divine Word, the Lutheran Confession, and our doctrine...The Calvinists teach an *absolute* election unto eternal life, and it is only after this election has been settled that God decrees to give faith to none but the elect. We, on the other hand, believe, teach, and confess according to the Scripture and our Confessions that God has ordained men *through faith* unto eternal life.[11]

However, this doctrine of the Scriptures and Confessions is not expressed by that conception which makes God's foreknowledge of faith to determine His choice in the elective act. The conception which embodies this view rather expresses the very opposite of what Scripture and the Confessions teach. If God has elected those whose perseverance in faith unto the end He foresaw, then faith is an antecedent of the eternal election, and not *pars ordinis electionis*. This conception which makes faith an antecedent of election pushes faith out of the elective act by placing it *ahead* of that act, while the Calvinistic conception, which yields a place to faith only in the execution of the divine decree, likewise removes faith from the elective act by placing it *after* that act. To keep up the appearances as though faith were retained as a part of eternal election, the patrons of the in-view-of-faith idea must call

---

[10] Cf. In Gen. 26, 9. Opp. exeg. lat. Erl. VI, 290 sqq.: Deus dicit tibi: En habes Filium meum, hunc audias et acceptes. Id si facis, jam certus es de fide et salute tua.... Audi Filium incarnatum et sponte se offeret praedestinatio.

[11] Berichtigung, 147.

in the aid of another fiction of human reasoning, *viz.*, they must construct a parallel between the divine act of election and the divine act of justification, thus converting an *operative* act of God into a *declaratory* one.

In another chapter (Chapter IX) we intend to show that not all who have espoused the term *intuitu fidei* have conceived of faith only as an *antecedent* of election, but have broken the force of the incorrect formula, because they have actually retained the Scripture doctrine regarding grace, and, particularly, because they have rejected the notion that a person's "right conduct" over and against divine grace furnishes us the explanation of the difficulty why some are converted and others not. By such teaching, the *intuitu fedei* is practically put out of commission, or, as someone expressed it: By teaching *sola gratia*, we practically pass the death-sentence on *intuitu fidei*. Practically, too, the doctrine that the believer is *certain* of his salvation and election serves to completely sidetrack that conception of election which posits foreseen, persevering faith as an antecedent of election. A person who is certain of his salvation and election has learned to disregard everything which God may have foreseen and presupposed, because no one can know what God may have foreseen concerning his person.

This is the favorable construction, a reconstruction rather, of the "second form." And here attention must be called to the fact that the Norwegian Agreement takes no cognizance of this favorable construction or recasting of the "second form," but accepts it *just as it reads*. The theses distinctly state that, according to the "second form," faith is an *antecedent* of election. As a result, not two "forms" of doctrine, but two doctrines, materially differing from one another, are presented in the theses. If a statement like this would occur in the theses: True, we employ this phrase that God has elected those of whom He foresaw that they would become believers and persevere in faith to the end, however, we mean by this foreknowledge of faith nothing but this that the believers are the elect, or that faith is part of the order of election,—I say, if the theses were to contain such a statement, they would not have placed another *doctrine* of Scripture and our Confessions, is the result. There is, indeed, also according to the Scriptures, "a decree of final glorification, with faith worked by the Spirit and perseverance as a necessary antecedent thereof." But this is not the decree of election taught in the Scriptures and in our Confessions, but *the judgement of the Last Day*.[12]

---

[12] Cf. Dr. Koren's contribution to Der Lutheraner, 1883, pp. 108 sq.

3

The Fundamental Difference

III. The Fundamental Difference

It would amount to concealing from oneself the true state of affairs, to assume that, by what is said in Theses 1 to 3 of the Madison Agreement about the two conceptions of election, the real difference has been brought to light which has hitherto separated the warring factions in the Lutheran Church of America. In the Articles of Agreement, which have been formulated after thirty years of controversy, the "first" and the "second form: for presenting the doctrine of Election are placed peaceably side by side. During the years of controversy they did not stand peaceably side by side, but stood in hostile opposition one against the other. The reason for this was that the "Second form" was, by its American advocates, used as a key with which they attempted to solve the *mystery* contained in the doctrines of Conversion and Election. The Madison Theses recognize this fact. They do not accept the "second form" unconditionally, but only permit it to stand side by side with the first, with the limitation, that it *must not be used in an effort to explain the mystery involved in the doctrine of Election*. For in Thesis 4 all "errors" are rejected which would attempt to explain "the mystery of election" on either synergistic or Calvinistic grounds.

Wherein, then, does this mystery consist? It would certainly have been in the interest for a clear presentation of the matter if Thesis 4 had been made to state *distinctly* wherein the mystery consists; for there are definitions of this mystery being circulated which are utterly at variance with one another. However, the matter involved in this mystery is indicated by reference to the respective paragraphs of the Formula of Concord. Paragraphs 39 to 44 of the Norwegian edition correspond to paragraphs 52 to 64 of Mueller's German edition of the Formula. Hence the mystery referred to in Thesis 4 is that described by the Formula of Concord as follows: "One is hardened, blinded, given over to a reprobate mind, while another, who is indeed in the same guilt, is again converted, etc." Thesis 4 of the Articles of Agreement, then, demands that no attempt be made to solve this mystery either on synergistic grounds, by a denial of *sola gratia*, or on Calvinistic grounds, by a denial of *gratia universalis*, but that it be acknowledged to be insoluble during our present life. Let us ascertain briefly in what respect we are facing a mystery at this point. The Scriptures teach, on the one hand, that the grace of God in Christ is extended to all men alike, and, on the other hand, that there is no difference among men, since all are in the same state of total depravity and in the same guilt before God, and their conduct over against the saving grace of God is equally evil. Such being the case, we might conclude, either that all men would be saved by the grace of God, or all men be lost by reason of their own guilt. Instead, the Scriptures teach that some are saved merely by the grace of God, and the rest are lost solely by their own guilt. Why this different result when the underlying conditions are the same? This is the mystery which no man ever has properly solved, and no man ever will properly solve in this life, because the Word of God offers no solution. We should bear in mind that no mystery appears when each of the classes, those who are finally saved, and those who are lost, are considered *separately*. In this separate view of the two classes everything is explained by the Word of God. The Word of God names only one cause of the conversion and final salvation of those actually converted and finally saved: it is in each and every instance the grace of God in Christ. Likewise it names only one cause of the non-conversion, and failure to be saved, of those who are not converted and not finally saved: it is in each and every instance the fault of man; it is owing, in particular, to his resistance against the converting operations of the Holy Spirit. The hardening of man's heart, too, proceeds only on the basis of human guilt. But the mystery appears when both classes are *compared with one another*. The question then arises: If grace is universal and total depravity general, then, why are not all converted and finally saved? Why some *rather than others*? *Cur alii prae aliis?* It is *this* question that the Word of God does not answer. At this point we must, with the Formula of Concord, acknowledge a mystery insoluble in this life. If a person so much as *strives* to solve this difficulty, he proves himself a poor theologian, because he does not know the limitations of theological knowledge: he presumes to know more in matters spiritual than is revealed in God's Word, while he who *actually solves* this mystery is forthwith proved a false teacher; for he denies either the *sola gratia*, that is, he denies that those who are saved are saved solely by the grace of God, or her denies *universalis gratia, i.e.*, he denies that all who are lost are lost by their own fault. We are bound, therefore, to acknowledge that we have before us a grand statement in these words of Thesis 4 of the Norwegian Agreement: "We have *agreed* to reject all erroneous doctrines which seek to explain away the mystery of Election either in a synergistic manner or a Calvinizing way." We call this a grand statement, because a glance into the history of the Church informs us that the great majority of well-known theologians in all ages have tried to solve this mystery, and have thereby run counter to the clear teaching of the Scriptures. In this matter even the great Augustine never fully gained the right balance. In his early life he offended against *sola gratia* by teaching synergism. For this he made amends in his *Retractationes*.[13] But later he encroached upon *universalis gratia*.[14] The right balance was recovered in 529 at the Synod of Arausio (Orange). The resolutions of this synod utter the correct Scriptural position; for they reject, on the one hand, the *praedestinatio ad malum*, and, on the other hand, they pursue into its farthest retreats, and refute by clear passages of Scripture, the error that faith and salvation have

---

[13] Cf. F. C., Mueller, p. 595, 27. Jacobs, p. 558.

[14] Cf. e.g., *Enchir. ad Laur.* c. 103; De corrept. et gratia c. 14.

any cause or motive in man.[15] However, in the Gottschalkian controversy on Predestination in the ninth century dense darkness again reigns on both sides. The one side has fallen into the ditch on the left, the other on the right side of the road. Gottschalk denied universal grace,[16] and his opponents (Hinkmar and others), who pretended to speak for the "Church," as clearly denied *sola gratia*, by teaching that man's free will after the Fall is not *dead* unto the good, but merely *imperfect (non emortuum, sed vitiatum)*. This party held that election unto everlasting life is conditioned upon God's foreknowledge of man's good behavior. Those who are lost might also have merited eternal life if they had so willed.[17] Pelagianism and Semipelagianism reigned throughout the Middle Ages until the Reformation. In the century of the Reformation again it was Melanchthon in his later years who with his followers solved the mystery by asserting a dissimilar conduct on the part of various men,–[18]that is to say, by denying *sola gratia*. Calvin gained the same end by denying universal grace.

---

[15] See Mansi, Amplissima Coll. Concil. VIII, 712 sqq. The most important of the 25 sections are cited in F. Pieper, *Die Grunddifferenz in der Lehre von der Bekehrung und Gnadenwahl*, pp. 34 sqq.

[16] Gottschalk: Ego Gotteschalcus credo et confiteor quod...illos omnes impios et peccatores, quos proprio fuso sanguine Filius Dei redimere venit, hos omnipotentis Dei bonitas ad vitam praedestinatos irretracribiliter salvari tantummodo velit; et rursum illos omnes impios et peccarores, *pro quibus idem Filius Dei nec corpus assumsit, nec orationem, ne dico sanguinem fudit, neque pro eis ullo modo crucifixus fuit*, quippe quos pessimos futuros esse praescivit, quesque justissime in aeterna praecipitandos tormenta praefinivit, ipsos omnio perpetim salvari penitus nolit. (See Gieseler, II, 1, p. 101; also Schmid, Dogmengeschichte, ed. by Hauck, p.227.)

[17] *Hinkmar*: Arbitrium liberum in primo homine *non fuit emortuum*, sed vitiatum, in nobis autem ad malum agendum arbitrium male est liberum...Ad bene agendum autem, imo et ad bene volendum tunc vere est nostrum arbitrium liberum, cum fuerit gratia liberatum, quod non est *resuscitatum* quia non fuit emortuum, sed gratia. est sanatum, quia vitio fuit corruptum. Et reprobi idcirco nequaquam coelestis patriae praemia aeterna percipient, quia ea nunc, dum promereri poterant, ex libero arbitrip contempserunt... Bonum quod agimus et Dei est et nostrum: Dei per praevenientem gratiam, nostrum per obsequentem liberam voluntatem. (Quoted by Schmid, 1. c., pp. 228 sq.)

[18] Loci, ed. by Detzer, I, 74: Cum promissio sit universalis, nec sint in Deo contradictoriae voluntates, necesse est, in nobis esse aliquam discriminis causam, cur Saul abjiciatur, David rescipiatur, id est, necesse est, aliquam esse actionem dissimilem in his duobus.

In the Eleventh Article of the Formula of Concord, in which conversion and salvation, on the one hand, has been so emphatically referred only to the grace of God in Christ, while non-conversion and damnation, on the other hand, have been referred with such clearness to the guilt and the resistance of men. Moreover, in this connection it is also stated more forcibly than ever before that the question why some are saved rather than others cannot be answered in this life, but involves an insoluble mystery, since a comparison of those who are saved with those who are lost reveals the fact that *there is no such thing as dissimilar conduct*, inasmuch as the former are guilty of the same evil conduct and are in the same condemnation as the latter.

Soon, however, a down-grade movement becomes noticeable again in the Lutheran Church as regards this clear perception of the above truth. In the 17th century Latermann and his companions, as well as Musaeus and his following, again present the synergistic solution by ascribing to man *before* his conversion a self-determination in favor of conversion or a "good conduct" over against grace. Only a part of the later theologians, such men as Calovius, Quenstedt, J. A. Osiander, still cling to the statement: There is no *arbitrium liberatum* prior to conversion, not even an *arbitrium liberatum* produced by the powers imparted by divine grace by means of which man may conduct himself properly towards grace or decide to accept it. We must, therefore, rest the entire matter with these two statements: Whoever is converted and finally saved owes it all to the grace of God, and whoever remains unconverted and is lost has no one to blame but himself.[19] However, even these theologians maintain this position only with great labor and difficulty, because they are entangled with that unfortunate formula of *intuitu fidei*, and occasionally their theological trains begin to jump the track.

If we proceed now to review conditions in the 19th century, we find Calvinists, such as Shedd, Hodge, and Boehl, insisting with the utmost energy on the Calvinistic solution of the mystery in election by denying universal grace. On the other hand, "conservative" and "Lutheran" theologians of Germany (Luthardt, Frank, Dieckhoff, and others) regard it as self-evident

---

[19] In another chapter the doctrine of the latter dogmaticians will be treated *in extenso*.

that all must see the necessity of applying the synergistic solution of the difficulty. They contend that the teaching of the Formula of Concord regarding *sola gratia* must suffer a "restriction" and must be "developed" in such a way that under the influence of divine grace man decides for his own conversion, and in the lat analysis conversion and salvation rest on a person's conduct. And now as to the state of affairs within the Lutheran Church in our own country, the theology which would "develop" the Lutheran Confessions was brought to America by the Iowa Synod. Its controversy with the Missouri Synod on the doctrines of Conversion and Predestination began in 1871. Retaining the *intuitu fidei*, the Iowa Synod maintained that in the last analysis conversion and salvation are dependent on man's conduct and man's self-determination. Iowa branded as Calvinists those who profess that there is a mystery contained in the *discretio personarum* or in the question why some are saved rather than others. Dr. Schmidt and the Ohio Synod since 1880 have taken the Iowa Synod's position with the strongest emphasis upon "right conduct" as the deciding factor, and with a more forcible denunciation of all who recognize the mystery of the *discretio personarum* as Calvinists. In the Missouri Synod's Thirteen Theses of 1881, the doctrinal position of the Formula of Concord was again given clear utterance. These theses maintain at every point both universal grace over against Calvinism and salvation "by grace alone" over against synergism, and accordingly, warn against either the Calvinistic or the synergistic solution of the mystery of election. The Norwegian Agreement in Section 4 likewise rejects "all erroneous doctrines which attempt to explain the mystery of election, either in a synergistic or a Calvinistic way." Section 5 is intended to exclude the synergistic, Section 6 the Calvinistic solution of the mystery. The fundamental difference, then, in the controversy consists in the acknowledgement or rejection of an insoluble mystery in the fact that "one is hardened, blinded, given over to a reprobate mind, while another, who is indeed in the same guilt, is again converted." As will be clear from a perusal of the following chapters, the Lutheran Church in America has had to deal only with *synergistic* attempts to solve this mystery.

4

An Injustice Done the Norwegian Synod

IV. An Injustice Done the Norwegian Synod by the Madison Agreement

The Calvinistic solution of the mystery is brought about by a denial of universal grace. If the gracious will of God does not extend to all men, a sufficient reason has been found why not all men believe and are saved. According to this view God never intended that all men should be saved. "There has never been a time," says De Beza, "nor is there such a time, nor will there ever be such a time, when God has had, or has, or will have compassion upon human beings individually."[20] Thus a difficulty has, indeed, been removed with which the understanding of man has ever wrestled; but those who have effected the removal have, by that same act, flatly contradicted the Scriptures, which clearly teach the universality both of God's grace in Christ and the efficient operation of the Spirit upon the hearts of all hearers. God would have all men to be saved ($\sigma\omega\theta\tilde{\eta}\nu\alpha\iota$).[21] The Son of God has given

---

[20] Response 2. *Ad. Acta Colloq. Mompelg.*, 194. See Quenstedt, II, 11. Calvin, Institutes. III, 22, 10. 11; 23, 1; 24, 15, 16.

[21] 1 Tim. 2:4.

Himself a ransom (ἀντίλυτρον) for all,[22] and testifies: I would have gathered you, but ye would not.[23] The Holy Spirit actively endeavors to enter also into the hearts of the stiff-necked (τῷ πνεύματι τῷ ἁγίῳ ἀντιπίπτετε).[24] Very properly, therefore, Section 6 of the Madison Theses *rejects* the doctrine that God passed by part of mankind with His earnest, gracious will, and that there are "two dissimilar redemptive wills" in God, one, efficient for conversion, which extends to the elect only, and another, non-efficient for conversion, which concerns the rest of humanity. This rebuttal of Calvinism is quite proper, since it is impossible to state comprehensively the Scriptural doctrine of Election, as distinguished from human error, without rejecting synergism on the one hand and Calvinism on the other. This method, accordingly, is adopted also in the Arausinian resolutions, in the Eleventh Article of the Formula of Concord and in the Thirteen Theses adopted at Fort Wayne.

Yet, there is something not in order in this rejection of Calvinism in Section 6 of the Articles of Agreement. An injustice is here done the Norwegian Synod if Section 6 is taken in connection with Section 4. The fourth section is introductory to the rejection of synergism (Sec. 5) and the rejection of Calvinism (Sec. 6), and reads as follows: "Since, however, during the controversy among us, words and expressions have been used—rightly or wrongly attributed to one party or the other—which seemed to the other side a denial of the Confession of the Church, or which at least might lead to such denial," etc. We have read these words time and again. But we cannot get any other impression than this: the theses leave it undecided whether the Norwegian Synod did not during the doctrinal controversy employ Calvinistic words and phrases, or attempt a Calvinistic solution of the mystery of election. But this does not agree with the facts in the case. If there is anything in this world like a historical fact, this is a historical fact, that the Norwegian Synod has at all times taught, clearly and without any reservation, the universality of God's earnest grace. There has not been a

---

[22] 1 Tim. 2:6.

[23] Matt. 23:37.

[24] Acts 7:51.

shred of Calvinism in the doctrinal position of the Norwegian Synod. But on what grounds? Not by fastening upon the Norwegian Synod terms and phrases in which it had denied universal grace, universal redemption, and the sufficiency of the work of the Holy Spirit, unto conversion upon the hearts of all hearers of the Word. All this the Norwegian Synod has ever maintained with great clearness, persistency, and precision. When the United Church leaders raised the charge of Calvinism, they based it upon the Norwegian Synod's unwillingness to accept the *synergistic* solution of the mystery of election; or, to state the matter more concretely: they based it upon the Norwegian Synod's teachings that conversion and salvation are the result of divine grace alone, and not also of man's conduct. Dr. Schmidt wrote: "In their confession the Norwegian Missourians have a *rejection-clause*[25] which reads thus: 'We reject as s*ynergistic* doctrine the teaching that...salvation *in a certain sense* does not depend upon God alone.'"[26] On the basis of this "rejection-clause" of the "Norwegian Missourians," that is to say, on the basis of their rejection of the *synergistic* error, that salvation does not rest upon the mercy of God alone, but also upon human conduct, Dr. Schmidt charges the Norwegian Synod with *Calvinism*, buttressing his charge with the notorious formula that all men would have to be saved if salvation rested with God alone. Again: The "Norwegian Missourians" took occasion to address to the Norwegian "Anti-Missourians" five test-questions, as follows: "1. Is it God alone who effects in man both a willingness to be converted, and also conversion itself? 2. It is God alone who takes away the inward, willful resistance of the heart against grace, in each instance where such resistance is taken away? 3. Is it God alone who not only gives man the power to be converted, but also effects the putting to use of such power? 4. Does man's conversion and salvation depend upon God alone? 5. Can and should a child of God be sure by faith of his final salvation?" Upon these questions Dr. Schmidt commented as follows: "Note especially the fourth question: 'Does man's conversion and salvation depend upon God alone?' This is the cardinal

---

[25] Italics our own.

[26] A. *u.* N. V, 334.

question among the five, yea, in a certain sense, the cardinal question of the whole controversy. The Missourians, of course, insist upon an unconditional affirmation of this question."[27] It is with this affirmation of the *sola gratia* by the "Norwegian Missourians" that Dr. Schmidt would establish his charge of Calvinism against them. To be brief, the Norwegian Synod had adhered to the *sola gratia* teaching, and had rejected that solution of the mystery in election which synergism attempts by its injection of a consideration of man's conduct. *The reason,* then, why the Norwegian Synod was charged with teaching Calvinism was, not because of any *Calvinistic* utterance which it had made, but because of its *antisynergistic* utterances, as indicated above.

Hence it is unfair, and evidently a glaring injustice is done to the Norwegian Synod, when Section 4 leaves it undecided whether the Norwegian Synod has not used Calvinistic terms and words during the controversy. The point at issue between the Norwegian synods was never the Calvinistic, but always the synergistic solution of the mystery of election. Dr. Schmidt admits as much when he declares the question of human conduct to be the cardinal question, "*Kernfrage,*" as he calls it, of the entire controversy. Nor should any doubt be expressed in Section 4 whether the other party to the controversy had made *synergistic* utterances. If that is synergism which is rejected in Section 5,—and that is indeed synergism,—then the other party has spoken the language of synergism. It has termed the "human conduct" rejected in Section 5 the "cardinal point" of the entire controversy, and on that account has charged the Norwegian Synod with Calvinism. In order to make clear that the difference has really been removed, and in order to avoid the misconception as if the Norwegian Synod had taught Calvinism as defined in Section 6, a statement should be added somewhat to this effect: "However, when we reject, in Section 5, every cause for conversion and salvation sought in man, especially in human conduct, either from natural or so-called spiritual powers,—that must not be made the ground for raising the charge of Calvinistic language or doctrine against us." This would clear the situation. Since the leaders of the United Church have accepted Section 5, they will no doubt *cheerfully*

---

[27] A. u. N.V, 332.

make this declaration. If there should be any who are not ready to give this declaration, this would be conclusive evidence that such have not at heart agreed to Section 5.

This is something worth remembering also for German and English Lutherans: If there is to be true unity among them in the doctrine of Conversion and Election, it must be universally avowed and conceded that no one is to be accused of *Calvinism* because he teaches the *sola gratia*, more specifically, because he rejects the "good conduct of man" over against converting and saving grace as a reason which explains that person's conversion, salvation, and election. Until this is clearly recognized and conceded, there cans be no thought of unity and peace. This point is discussed more fully in the following chapter.

5

Madison Theses and the Rejection of Synergism

V. The Madison Theses and the Rejection of Synergism.

The synergistic solution of the mystery of election is brought about by a denial of *sola gratia*. It is immaterial how much one subtracts from divine grace. If conversion and salvation do not rest upon divine grace alone, but in some measure upon man himself, upon his "good conduct," upon anything good that man does, or upon anything evil that he omits to do, the problem why only a part of humanity becomes converted and saved is made clear to human reason. In this case only some men have—by acting or not acting—contributed the necessary share required of man toward effecting conversion. Thus the difficulty in the path of human understanding is fully removed, but at the same time a contradiction with the Scriptures is created. A contradiction, in the first place, with all the texts which describe the state of natural man. According to these texts there is no difference among men. There is no part of mankind, no, not a single human being, which maintains the "right attitude" over against grace. *Every* man is by nature not only dead (νεκρός) in sins,[28] but is filled with enmity against the Gospel: he regards the Gospel as foolishness (μωρία),[29] and resists grace until *God* has changed his heart and will.[30] In the second place, a contradiction is created with regard to all those texts that ascribe to the working of God's grace and omnipotence alone the effects of conversion and final salvation. We believe according to the working of His mighty power.[31] We are kept by the power of God through faith unto salvation.[32] It is not of him that willeth, nor of him that runneth, but of God that showeth mercy.[33] If there is a thought which all Christians reject as a suggestion of the devil and as a lapse from faith, it is the thought that the fact of their conversion is to be explained by good conduct on their part over against grace. Hence it is the purpose of Section 5 of the Madison Theses *to reject* the synergistic solution of the mystery of election.

Does Thesis 5 really accomplish this? Or may synergists rightly claim that their doctrine is set forth in Section 5? This thesis has been viewed in two ways within the camp of those who hitherto waged war against the Norwegian Synod and ourselves. Some have regarded it as acceptable, others not. Which party is supported by the facts in the case? Manifestly the latter, which rejects Section 5. In all subdivisions of this section, synergism, as it has appeared in the American Lutheran Church, is excluded. This is done already in Subdivision a, where, in the language of the Formula of Concord, the doctrine is rejected, "that God's mercy and the most holy merits of Christ are not the sole reason for our election, but that there is also *in ourselves* a cause for such election, for the sake of which God has ordained us to eternal life. Even in this place the notion of "right conduct" on the part of man is dismissed; for, surely, right conduct on the part of man is something *in man*. More than this: In the following subdivision of Section 5 right

---

[28] Eph. 2:1, 5.

[29] 1 Cor. 2:14.

[30] John 6:43-45.

[31] Eph. 1:19-20.

[32] 1 Pet. 1:5.

[33] Rom. 9:16.

or good conduct on the part of man is expressly rejected as the ground of explanation for a person's conversion, and that, not only such conduct as a person is able to render by his natural powers, but also such conduct as results from what are called powers imparted by the Spirit. Hence it is clear that no Iowan, no Ohioan, nor Dr. Schmidt and his followers can find, in Section 5, any approval or tolerance of the position hitherto maintained by them. For all these parties have not only made casual mention of the "conduct" that is here rejected, but they have persistently and with one accord maintained that this "conduct" is the "cardinal question" and the principal matter in their controversy with us. They have persistently, and with one accord, insisted that there is absolutely no way of getting along without this element of man's "conduct" is the "cardinal question" and the principal matter in their controversy with us. They have persistently, and with one accord, insisted that there is absolutely no way of getting along without this element of man's "conduct" in any presentation of the doctrine of conversion and Election. This human conduct they have held to be the only means of steering clear of Calvinism. And because the Norwegian Synod and the Synodical Conference *rejected* man's conduct as the ground of explanation for a person's conversion and final salvation, they have seized upon this rejection to justify their emphatic, unanimous, and persistent charge of Calvinism against us.

After writing on this topic for more than a quarter of a century, it is with a feeling of reluctance that we take up the task of pointing out this fact again and again and of submitting the respective utterances for publication. Such procedure, however, serves to clarify the situation, and thus may aid in establishing an honest peace. The question of human conduct has been termed "the cardinal question of the entire controversy."[34] It is "undeniable that in a certain respect conversion and final salvation are dependent upon man and not upon God alone."- "We consider it un-Christian and heathenish to say that the actual attainment of that salvation which has been perfectly provided and earnestly intended for all men is not in any respect dependent upon man's conduct over against this salvation, but in every respect upon

---

[34] *A.u.N.V*, 332.

the grace of God alone."³⁵ "One would suppose that even a blind Missourian could still comprehend this much, *viz.*, that he puts himself in a precarious condition by maintaining the thesis that man's conversion and salvation are dependent upon God alone—exclusive of all consideration of man's conduct over against the effectual calling, quickening, and working of the grace of God."³⁶ "This thesis"—that man's conversion and salvation are dependent alone on the grace of God and in no wise upon human conduct— "is the real quintessence of the whole Calvinism concept of Election."³⁷ And because it is supposed to be "undeniably" true that the converting and saving grace of God is regulated by the good conduct of man or man's self-determination, there is no longer any such mystery as the Formula of Concord speaks of in §§57–64, this mystery, to wit: "One is hardened, blinded, and given over to a reprobate mind, while another, who is indeed in the same guilt, is again converted." To assert a mystery here is "Calvinism." "The dissimilar workings of converting and saving grace are well explained on the ground of the dissimilar conduct of men over against grace."³⁸ Nor can the means of grace effect conversion and conserve faith without the superaddition of man's good conduct. "The actual final result of the means of grace depends not only upon the sufficiency and efficacy of the means themselves, but also upon the conduct of man in regard to the necessary condition of passiveness and submissiveness under the Gospel call."³⁹ As surely as the above-cited utterances express the doctrine of the opponents of the Norwegian Synod and the Synodical Conference, so certain it is that this doctrine of theirs is condemned in Section 5 of the Madison Agreement.

At its last convention the Synodical Conference voiced the desire that in Section 5 the cessation of willful resistance before conversion, as a determinative factor in conversion and election, be rejected. This does

---

[35] *Zeitblaetter*, 1887, 325.

[36] *Kirchenzeitung*, 1885, 76.

[37] *Zeitblaetter*, 1888, 144.

[38] *Zeitblaetter*, 1911, 526.

[39] Lutheran Standard, February 28, 1891.

not raise a new issue, but merely emphasizes a particular species of "good conduct" which our opponents have employed in teaching the dependence of conversion upon man's cooperation. The Norwegian Synod has frequently and emphatically declined this very notion of the cessation of willful resistance as the ground of explanation for a person's conversion and election.[40] The second of the five test-questions submitted to Dr. Schmidt by the "Norwegian Missourians" reads: "Is it God alone who takes away the willful resistance of the heart against grace, in every instance where it is taken away?"[41]

However, objection must be made to a few words in the rejection of synergism in Section 4. Reference there is made to "man's sense of responsibility in respect of the acceptance or rejection of God's grace." Judging from the context, it appears that this expression is intended to urge the universal and earnest grace of God (*gratia sufficiens*) as extending to *all* hearers of the Word, and thus to bring out strongly the fact that man's failure to be converted must in each instance be charged to his own account. However, the clause says not only this, but more than this. The words read as if man stood in like relation to the *acceptance* as to the *rejection* of grace. As a matter of fact, however, acceptance and rejection of grace proceed from "*dissimilar* principles" as the later theologians urged against Latermann's position. Rejection of grace is purely a work of *man*, acceptance of grace purely a work of *God*. The phrase, "feeling of responsibility over against the acceptance or rejection of grace," creates the impression as if there existed in man before his conversion a condition or a moment of time in which he may decide, as well whether he will accept, as whether he will reject, the grace offered him. This notion, however, is, quite properly, rejected with much emphasis in Section 5.

No objection can be raised to the term in Section 5d where we read that man, before his conversion, has no energy conveyed by the call of grace, and therefore "indwelling in him or belonging to him." This expression was

---

[40] L&W. 1884, p. 181.

[41] A.u.N.V, 332.

used in the 17th century against Latermann, and has been used also by the Missouri Synod to ward off a twofold error: 1) the error involved in teaching that previous to conversion there are no motions (*motus*) whatever effected in the human heart by the Spirit of God, which is contrary to the Scriptures and to the Scriptural terminology in vogue in our Church; and 2) the false assumption of a *status medius*, which takes for granted that man even before his conversion is no longer spiritually dead, but in part has commenced to be spiritually alive, his will being no longer full of enmity against the Gospel, but in a measure favorably inclined to its call. The chapter on the "preparations for Conversion" will deal more fully with this point.

6

Conversion by Means of "New Powers Imparted by Grace"

VI. Conversion "by Means of New Powers Imparted by Grace."

Thesis 5d of the Norwegian Agreement rejects the doctrine that faith is the resultant of a power *"imparted by the call of grace,"* enabling man to decide for grace. Is this rejection justifiable? If real unity is to be attained in the American Lutheran Church with reference to the doctrine of Conversion and Election, an understanding must first be reached concerning the phraseology frequently employed in former centuries as well as in our own day, *viz.*, that man is converted (converts himself) by means of "powers offered or imparted to him by grace"; specifically, that by means of powers so conferred he decides for conversion, conducts himself rightly over against grace, ceases to resist willfully, etc. At the first glance many may regard this mode of speaking as altogether void of design. It seems to render all honor to God, and seemingly excludes all cooperation on the part of man, as he is by nature, in his conversion. However, this impression is specious. In reality, this phraseology has been invented and employed for the purpose of covering up the actual state of affairs. What is intended by the phrase, "powers imparted by grace," never denotes, in reality, powers of grace, but *natural* powers. That is the sense connected with this phrase both by those who employed it in the 16th and 17th centuries, and by those who have used it in the 19th and who are now using it in the 20th century. Schmauk is quite right in saying: "Man's will is able to decide for salvation through new powers bestowed by God. This is the *subtle synergism* which has infected nearly the whole of modern Evangelical Protestantism, and which is, or has been, taught in institutions bearing the name of our Church."[42] Just so Walther: "All these ingenious fabrications, *viz.*, those notions of persons conducting themselves rightly, or deciding in favor of divine grace, by means of '*Gnadenkraefte*,' have no other purpose than to dissolve the mystery that man is saved by grace alone, and is damned through his own fault."[43]

Keep this in mind: previous to his conversion, or before the light of faith is kindled in his heart, man is spiritually *dead*, and can, previous to his conversion, *employ* the spiritual powers offered in God's gracious call as little as one who is physically dead can employ the physical vitality if it were offered him. If, notwithstanding this, the ability to apply spiritual powers imparted to man, for determining his attitude, or for correctly conducting himself toward the gracious offer of God, is attributed to him prior to his conversion, or regeneration, that amounts to attributing to him at least so much of *natural* moral powers that he is able *rightly to employ* the spiritual powers offered him. This fact was very ably set forth by Dr. Stellhorn in 1872 over against Iowa. The Iowaans, too, made use of this mode of speaking, *viz.*, that a self-determination, or right conduct, for conversion is made possible through the *spiritual* powers offered to man by God. Dr. Stellhorn wrote: "According to this doctrine, natural man *only lacks powers*; he is, as it were, a fettered prisoner who desires to be free, or who, *in his natural state*, at least *may* be found to possess a will or desire to be saved in the right manner, and to decide for God; he has, by nature, or at least may have, the right inclination and quality of the will, and only lacks the *powers* for deciding as he desires,

---

[42] The Confessional Principle, 1911, 752.

[43] L&W, 1872, p. 294.

or, to say the least, is able to desire. I hold that this is attributing too much to natural man. He does not only lack the *power* to will or do what is good, but he—or, what comes to the same, his will—has an *inclination or nature* which is radically wrong. And so long as this is the case, all powers offered him can profit him nothing. For by reason of this nature or inclination [of his will] it would never occur to him to employ said powers towards doing or willing that which is good."[44] Dr. Stellhorn, accordingly, declares that this Iowaan doctrine of a decision in favor of the Gospel, rendered possible to man by powers imparted to him by grace, is a doctrine at variance with Holy Writ, "because it militates *in defectu* against the Biblical doctrine or original depravity," *i.e.*, it does not say enough about that depravity, because it does not regard natural man as being *dead* in sins, but predicates of him a *natural quality* which permits him, while still unconverted, rightly to employ the powers proffered by grace.

By this same argument Lutheran theologians in the 17th century succeeded in making clear their objection to the teaching of Latermann. Latermann, too, while conceding that man by nature resists the Gospel, formulated his teaching so as to declare that under the influence of the Gospel man may decide for conversion *by means of powers which grace offers to him*. The theologians pointed out the self-deception involved in this formula, since Latermann evidently assumed in man *before* his conversion the existence of *natural* "good powers" by means of which man is enabled to employ rightly the powers offered by grace. The Straussburg faculty declared: "Latermann's utterances are ambiguous and confused. For what sort of power is that because of which it rests with man by means of grace to do, or not to do, that which is necessary for conversion? with which it rests to desire conversion, or not to desire it, to use Latermann's expressions? He cannot say that this is the power and ability *conferred by the Holy Spirit*. For what manner of statement would this be: 'It rests with the *new* powers and abilities imparted by the Holy Spirit to perform, or not to perform, what is necessary for conversion, to be, or not to be, converted'! Are these new powers, then, *indifferent* as

---

[44] *Monatshefte*, 1872, pp. 346-348.

to conversion or aversion, as to inclination or declination? Accordingly, there must be *in man, previous* to the impartation of spiritual gifts through the Holy Ghost, an ability which by the aid of supervening grace performs what is necessary unto conversion, and by means of which the inclination to become converted is produced. And this is Pelagianism and synergism."[45] The Strassburg faculty was altogether right. In every instance where it is claimed that *before* his conversion man determines himself for, or assumes a right attitude toward, the powers of grace offered him, there are ascribed to man in his *natural* state good powers by means of which he is well able to make the right use of the proffered powers of grace. This position assumes that man in his unconverted state has a *natural facultas se applicandi ad gratiam,* which is merely roused into action (*excitatur*) under the sound of the Word.

However, it becomes evident in still another way that in the statement: Man conducts himself correctly by means of the grace of God, the intended meaning is that man does so, not by the grace of God, but by his *natural* powers, by some good quality naturally inherent in him. For this conduct is made to explain the mystery why some are converted and others not. "The dissimilar conduct of men over against grace,"[46] according to a statement made quite recently, "well *explains* the dissimilar working of converting, saving grace." Conduct resulting from grace alone would explain nothing, since the powers offered by grace are offered to those who remain unconverted, as well as to those who became converted. The instance upon conduct as an *explanation* is positive proof that not spiritual, but natural powers are meant. As stated before: if an understanding is to be reached among the Lutherans in America with reference to the doctrine of Conversion and Election, we must not even *for the sake of the argument* concede that men *mean* powers of grace when they *speak* of powers of grace. What men have meant to express in the past, and still mean to express at present, by such phraseology is a conduct of man that is owing to his natural powers. Thus there is assumed in man, as he is by nature, a cause—and that, the cause which ultimately turns the

---

[45] Apud. Calov, X, p. 50.

[46] Zeitblaetter, 1911, p. 526.

scale and decides the matter—for his own conversion, salvation, and election. The same idea is expressed *in a very direct manner* when grace and human conduct are put in opposition to each other, as is done in the oft-repeated assertion that conversion and salvation do not depend on God's grace alone, but also upon man's right conduct.

7

The Point of Difference Stated by the Formula

VII. The Point of Difference as Stated by the Formula of Concord.

Our Christian church-folk, to be sure, are expected to exercise considerable critical acumen when they are to recognize he error hidden under the expression that man conducts himself rightly, so as to bring about his own conversion, "by means of powers which grace offers him." If a method of presenting this matter could be devised which would entirely dispense with the discussion concerning "dissimilar conduct" from "natural" or "spiritual powers," that method surely ought to receive a royal welcome. Well, there is such a method. Nor do we need to go in search of such a method; for it is presented in our Lutheran Confessions. Our Confession declares that *there is no such thing as "dissimilar conduct"* when those who are converted and saved are *compared* with those who remain unconverted and are lost. When those who are saved and compared with those who are lost, dissimilar conduct is found to be a *non-ens*—something which does not exist in actual fact. For does not our Confession say expressly that we who are converted and saved do not conduct ourselves better, but

THE POINT OF DIFFERENCE STATED BY THE FORMULA

quite as badly (as the rest), and are "in the same guilt?"[47]

In reference to those who are finally saved, or the elect, our Confession makes a twofold statement: 1) when it *describes* the temporal aspect of the elect without inquiring into the reason for the difference, or 2) when it *compares* the elect with those who are lost in such a manner that the differential cause comes up for discussion. Regarding the first statement, our Confession says that those who are saved conduct themselves quite differently from those who are lost and rejected. This different mode of conduct is extensively treated in the paragraphs dealing with the question, "Whence, and by what token, can we know who are the elect?"[48] While those who are finally lost "despite the Word of God, reject, calumniate, and persecute it, or, when they hear it, harden their hearts, resist the Holy Ghost, without repentance persevere in sins, do not truly believe in Christ, only present [godliness in] an outward appearance, or seek other ways for righteousness and holiness apart from Christ,"[49] the elect, or saved, on the contrary, show a different conduct: "they hear the Gospel, believe in Christ, pray and five thanks, are sanctified in love, have hope, patience, and comfort under the cross, and although in them all this is very weak, yet they hunger and thirst for righteousness."[50] So different, indeed, so contrary, is the conduct of those who will be finally saved to the conduct of the lost, when each class is considered separately, *i. e.,* without asking for the cause of this difference. There is an altogether different tenor in what the Confessions say when they enter upon a discussion of the fact that "God gives His Word at one place, but not at another, removes it from one place, and allows it to remain at another; also, that one is hardened, blinded, given over to a reprobate mind, while another is again converted"—hence, when they inquire into the cause of the difference, why some are converted and saved, and others are not converted and not saved, and with this point in view institute a *comparison* of the two classes of mankind, the saved and the lost, *as*

---

[47] Mueller, p. 716, §§57-59. Jacobs, p. 659.

[48] F.C. Art. XI, §§25 sqq. Jacobs, p. 653.

[49] Mueller, p. 712 §39. Jacobs, p. 656.

[50] Mueller, p. 710 §30, Jacobs, p. 655.

to their conduct toward God's Word and His grace. Here the Confession does *not* assert with Iowa, Ohio, and Dr. Schmidt: "The *dissimilar conduct* of man, then, toward the converting, saving grace explains the dissimilar workings of such grace"; *on the contrary*, the Confession devotes eight paragraphs to a demonstration of the fact that there is *no dissimilar conduct,* but conduct *exactly similar.* Those who are finally saved were "in the same guilt," have also "conducted themselves evilly over against the Word of God." True, even at this point the Confession maintains that those who will be lost are lost not, indeed, by reason of some lack of grace in God, but through their own guilt, having conducted themselves evilly over against the Word of God. But those who are finally saved are not saved because they conducted themselves "differently" or better than those who will be lost, but "placed alongside of them and compared with them" (Latin: *quam simillimi illis deprehensi*) "being found entirely similar unto them," they may learn the more attentively to recognize and praise God's pure unmerited grace." This entire section of eight paragraphs (57-64) of the Formula of Concord is a *protest* against the assumption upon which our opponents are standing, the assumption, namely, that there is a dissimilar conduct on the part of man over against grace, and that the dissimilar working of converting, saving grace is thereby explained. By all means, read those paragraphs; they are as follows:

"Likewise when we see that God gives His Word at one place, but not at another; removes it from one place, and allows it to remain at another; also, that one is hardened, blinded, given over to a reprobate mind, while another, *who is indeed in the same guilt*, is again converted, etc.: in these and similar questions Paul fixes before us a certain limit as to how far we should go, *viz.*, that in the one part we should recognize God's judgement. For they are richly deserved penalties of sins when God so punishes a land or nation for despising His Word, that the punishment extends also to their posterity as is to be seen in the Jews. Thereby God shows to those that are His, His severity in some lands and persons, in order to indicate *what we all have richly deserved, since we have acted wickedly in opposition to God's Word,* and often have sorely grieved the Holy Ghost; so that we may live in God's fear and acknowledge and praise *God's goodness* in and with us *without, and contrary to, our merit*, to whom He gives and grants His Word, and whom He does not harden and reject. For inasmuch as our nature has been corrupted by sin, and is worthy of, and under obligation to, God's wrath and condemnation, God owes to us neither Word, Spirit, nor grace; and when, out of grace, He bestows these gifts, *we often repel them from us, and judge ourselves unworthy of everlasting life*, Acts 13, 46. Therefore this His righteous, richly deserved judgement He displays in some countries, nations, and persons in order that, when we are considered with respect to them and compared with them" (Latin: *quam simillimi illis deprehensi,* found to be entirely like unto them), "we may learn the more attentively to recognized praise God's pure ad unmerited grace in the vessels of mercy. For no injustice is done those who are punished and receive the wages of their sins; but in the rest, to whom God gives and preserves His Word, and thereby enlightens, converts, and preserves men, God commends His *pure grace and mercy* without their merit. When we proceed thus far in this article, we remain upon the right way, as it is written: 'O Israel, thou hast destroyed thyself, but in me is thy help,' Hos. 13, 9. But with respect to that in this disputation which will proceed too high and beyond these limits, we should with Paul place the finger upon our lips and remember and say: 'O man, who are thou that repliest against God?' For that in this article we neither can nor should inquire after and investigate everything, the great apostle Paul declares. For when, after having argued much concerning this article from the revealed Word of God, he comes to where he points out what, concerning this mystery, God has reserved for His hidden wisdom, he suppresses and cuts off the discussion with the following words: 'O the depth of the riches both of the wisdom and knowledge of God! How unsearchable are His judgements, and His ways past finding out! For who hath known the mind of the Lord?'—that is, in addition to and beyond that which He has revealed in His Word."

Every reader *must* observe, from the foregoing statement of the Confession, that according to the Lutheran Confession there is no such thing as "dissimilar conduct of men" over against grace by which the dissimilar working of grace might be explained. Consequently, this whole argument is superseded, *viz.,* whether conduct is simply *non ens*. And it is for this very reason, because there is no unlike human conduct over against grace, that our Confession declares it to be a *mystery* why "one is hardened, blinded, given over to a reprobate mind, while another, who is indeed in the same guilt, is again converted."

By inculcating the non-existence of "dissimilar conduct," the Formula of Concord also puts an end to the game of blind man's buff which has been played with the word "mystery." The Confession continually points out the presence of a mystery in the doctrine of Conversion and Election. Naturally, one who does not agree with the Confession, but tries to make himself and others believe that he does agree with it, will endeavor to find some sort of mystery somewhere. For this purpose the "psychological" mystery was invented during the controversy. Just recently these parties said: "The mystery is there, and we cannot clear it up, but we can and should know where it lies, and where it is to be found. It is a psychological mystery, not a theological one. That is to say, it does not reside in God, and His will and working, but in the soul of man. We cannot understand, when the grace of God does all—short of compelling man—that is really necessary for his conversion, how it is that man can resist so maliciously and persistently as to render it impossible for God to convert him.[51] Whoever accepts this "psychological mystery," will find the mystery in the incomprehensible malice and baseness of those who will be lost. It is clear, however, that this is not the "mystery" which the Formula of Concord has in mind, since our Confession finds exactly the same malice and baseness among those who will finally be saved, as among those who will be lost: the same guilt, the same evil conduct, the same image, *quam simillimi illis deprehensi.*

---

[51] *Zeitblaetter*, 1912, p. 131.

8

Assent of All Christians to the Presentation

VIII. Assent of all Christians to the Presentation of Doctrine Made by the Formula of Concord.

The presentation which the Formula of Concord makes of the doctrines of Conversion and Election leaves no room for the notion of "dissimilar conduct" on the part of those who are saved, and those who are lost, when these are compared with one another. The first advantage accruing from this presentation of doctrine is, that we are relieved of the necessity of investigating whether good or "right" conduct is ascribed to "natural" or "spiritual" powers. It offers, however, another, and a greater advantage. The presentation of the Formula of Concord has the assent of all Christians, and of all theologians in so far as they are Christians. The Formula of Concord speaks the language of every Christian heart. It expresses the innermost conviction not only all of *Lutheran* Christians, whether of Norwegian, German, or English tongue, but *of all Christians on earth*. Christian faith, *i.e.,* faith in the grace of God's for Christ's sake, may exist in the midst of perversions and weaknesses. But there is *one* thing which precludes the beginning and the continuing of faith: the attitude of those who imagine that they are better *in the sight of God* than others, and who find in this fact the explanation why they have become, and remain, children of God. Faith cannot exist jointly with such an attitude of the heart. By the example of the Pharisee, in Luke 18, the Holy Spirit invites all Christians to the end of time to a view of this fact. The Pharisee thanks God that he is not like other men, extortioners, unjust, adulterers, or even as yonder publican. In this difference between himself and others the Pharisee finds the explanation why he is accepted of God, while the publican and the rest are rejected from God's presence. But according to the words of Christ, the reason given by the Pharisee is the very reason why the Pharisee went unjustified to his home, and was outside the pale of the Church, *extra ecclesiam*. This same attitude of the heart has worked harm for Israel according to the flesh. Israel could not attain to faith, but took offense at the corner-stone, Christ, because it claimed a preference over other persons and nations. Hence the warnings of Paul, directed to the Gentile Christians, lest they become guilty of the same fatal error. He admonishes them not to find an explanation why Israel was rejected and they themselves were engrafted by assuming a better conduct on their part as compared with the unbelieving and hardened Jews. If they should be ensnared by the same delusion, exalt themselves boastfully against the Jews, and thus fail to "continue in His goodness" (χρηστότης), they would also be cut off.[52] In short, there is not a single Christian in the world today, there has never in time past been a Christian, and there will never be a Christian until the Day of Doom who, as such, would explain his adoption to sonship with God by a reference to better conduct, on his part, in comparison with others. Faith will permit no such attitude, since faith, once for all time, is of such a nature that it "reposes on grace alone," as the Apology declares.[53]

At this point we American Lutherans can all come to an agreement, because it is the point on which, as Christians, we *already are agreed*. The Iowaans, in so far as they are christians, have never believed what they have maintained

---

[52] Rom. 11:17-22.

[53] Mueller, p. 97, §56.

against us since the early seventies, to wit, that conversion and salvation must be ultimately ascribed to man's self-determination or to his conduct. The Iowaans, as Christians, have ever believed the very opposite, expressed by them elsewhere, *e.g.,* when they wrote: "The entire Reformation was in reality nothing but a thousand-voiced anthem on the theme *soli Deo gloria*. And this consciousness, that the believer owes his salvation solely to the free grace of God in Christ, was the divine power which vanquished popery and the Roman Church."[54] Dr. Schmidt, too, as a Christian, has never believed what he has written since 1880, namely, that it is an "altogether dreadful doctrine" to make the conversion and salvation of man dependent on God alone, without taking cognizance of man's conduct.[55] Rather, as a Christian, Dr. Schmidt has always believed what he wrote in 1874 in rejection of the Iowaan notion of "self-determination": "Our earnest opposition to the theory of self-determination exhibited and defended by Prof. G. Fritschel in Brobst's *Monatshefte*, should astonish no one, as this doctrine ultimately transfers the miraculous work of conversion from the hand of God into the hand of man, and thus divests if of its real mystery. To render less profound the impenetrable mystery of Conversion and Election, by means of rationalizing speculation, here as with all mysteries of God, amounts to no more nor less than, in effect, demonstrating the mystery as such out of existence. We insist upon retaining the 'mystery of faith' also in this instance 'in order not to be defrauded; for it is not unknown to us what he really has in mind.'"[56] Nor has any Ohioan, as a Christian, ever believed what has been maintained by the Ohio Synod since 1881 regarding human conduct, *e. g.,* "Thus converting, saving grace is regulated by the conduct, over against it, of men," or, "Thus the dissimilar working of converting, saving grace is explained by the dissimilar conduct of men over against it." On the contrary, every Ohioan, as a Christian, has ever believed what his Synod confessed with reference to the mystery in conversion in the year 1875. A thesis had been submitted which located

---

[54] *Monatshefte*, 1872, p.48.

[55] A.u.N.V, p.332.

[56] L&W, 1874, p.39.

the mystery practically in the incomprehensible wickedness of the human heart. The Ohio Synod voiced its dissent, and declared that the mystery "rather consisted in the fact that one is roused, through the divine call of grace, from his sleep of sin, receives the faith, remains therein, and is finally saved, while another also hears the call of God, but does not arise, or if he rises, falls again from the faith, and is finally lost. The cause of our eternal salvation rests entirely in the grace of God; the cause of damnation, in the resistance of man against the operations of divine grace…It will ever remain an unsearchable mystery to human reason why God permits so many to be lost, when He earnestly desires that all should be saved. The Synod finally agreed to substitute for this thesis a paragraph from the Formula of Concord which states this difficult matter with incomparable clearness, and which reads as follows: 'For no injustice is done those who are punished and receive the wages of their sins; but in the rest, to whom God gives and preserves His Word, and thereby enlightens, converts, and preserves men, God commends His pure grace and mercy, without their merit.'"

How now? Is it possible for a person to speak and write otherwise in public than he believes in his heart before God? It is, indeed. Luther calls attention to this fact in *De Servo Arbitrio*. This is the way Luther explains it: The saints are entirely different persons *"inter disputandum,"* when they speak or write in public, from what they are when they come before God in their closet to pray and deal with their God. In public they attribute to man an ability to conduct himself rightly over against grace (*vim, quae ad gratiam sese applicat*); but as soon as they step before God, they *completely* forget (*penitus obliti*) their own ability, despair of themselves, sit down with all other men on the same mourner' bench, and cry for grace (*desperantes de semet ipsis ac nihil nisi solam et puram gratiam* LONGE ALIA MERITIS *incocantes*), saying with St. Bernard on his death-bed; I have lived wickedly, *perdite vixi*. But whence this dualism, this twofold system of bookkeeping? Its origin must be sought in the conflicting interests maintained before God and before the public. In public controversy men seek to gain victories *before men* (*verbis et disputationibus intenti sunt*): they feel obliged to maintain a position once assumed, to indulge an old or recent grudge, to cultivate an old or a new friendship. As soon, however, as they come before God, the Christian mind (*affectus*) which dwells in them asserts itself, and according to this mind they do not boast of their own conduct, but indict the same as being *purely hostile* to God and His Word. Now, Luther continues, believers as well as unbelievers should be judged rather on the basis of their real disposition than from their utterances.[57] In like manner Chemnitz points out the agreement of the Christians of every age and clime with the Lutheran doctrine of *Justification*. This agreement does not so much appear in public speech and argument—where they mingle works and human merit with Justification—as "in the serious exercise of repentance and faith, when an afflicted conscience, and the tribunal of God or in the agony of death, struggles with its own unworthiness."[58] The same applies to the Church in general, and, in particular, to the American Lutheran Church, with reference to the *sola gratia* in the doctrine of Conversion and Election. In public writings and disputations a "better conduct" of some men over against grace is taught, in an effort to explain the fact that not all men are finally

---

[57] *Opp. lat.* v. a. VII, 166: Si ex omnibus assertoribus liberi arbitrii ostendere potestis unum, qui tantillum robur animi vel affectus habuerit, ut in nomine et virtute liberi arbitrii unum obolum contemnere, uno bolo carere, unum verbum vel signum iniuriae ferre potuerit (nam de contemptu opum, vitae, famae nihil dicam), iterum palmum habete et sub hastam libenter ibimus. Atque id ipsum vos, qui tanta bucca verborum vim liberi arbitrii iactatis, nobis exhibere debetis, aut iterum de lana caprina videbimini statuere, aut ut ille in vacuo theatro ludos spectare. Ego vero contrarium vobis facile ostendam, quod viri sancti, quales iactatis, quoties ad Deum oraturi vel acturi accedunt, quam penitus obliti incedant liberi arbitrii sui, *desperantes de semet ipsis, ac nihil nisi solam et puram gratiam longe alia meritis sibi invocantes*, qualis saepe Augustinus, qualis Bernardus, cum moriturus diceret: Perdidi tempus meum, quia perdite vixi. Non video hic allegari vim aliquam, quae ad gratiam sese applicet, sed accusari omnem vim, quod *non nisi aversa fuerit*. Quanquam illi ipsi sancti aliquando inter disputandum aliter de libero arbitrio locuti sunt, sicut video omnibus acidisse ut alii sint, *dum verbis aut disputationibus intenti sunt*, et alii dum affectibus et operibus; illic *dicunt* aliter quam *affecti* fuerunt ante, hic aliter *afficiuntur* quam *dixerunt* ante. Ex affectu vero potuis, quam ex sermone metiendi sunt homines, tam pii quam impii.

[58] Chemnitz, *Examen*, De justificatione, p. 144: Haec pauca (from the patristic writings) ideo annotavi, ut ostenderem, doctrinam nostram de justificatione habere testimonia omnium piorum, qui omnibus temporibus fuerunt, idque non in declamatoriis rhetoricationibus nec in otiosis disputationibus, sed in seriis exercitiis poenitentiae et fidei, quando conscientia in tentationibus cum sua indignitate vel coam ipso judicio Dei vel in agone mortis luctatur.

saved. When the same persons, however, come before God and deal with Him, they not only forget the "better conduct" defended in public, but reject it as rubbish. This cannot be branded as judging of hearts, since the Scriptures themselves pass this judgement when they describe Christian faith as a faith resting on grace alone and not on human conduct. Our older dogmaticians have frequently adopted the method to conclude their argument for the correctness of Lutheran doctrine by the proof drawn from "the testimony of the opponents" (*e testimonio adversariorum*). And this procedure is perfectly proper. Everything that is at all Christian ultimately agrees with Lutheran doctrine, either expressly or in principle. So with reference to *universalis gratia*. Chapters 21-24 in Book III of Calvin's *Institutiones* are, in contents and manner, a great inventive against the foolishness of people who believe that the grace of God in Christ is *universal*. But in times of stress, when an affrighted conscience desires the comfort of divine grace, also the Calvinists, *by their own admission*,[59] must take recourse to the general promises of grace. And so with reference also to *sola gratia*. Here in America the "blind Missourians" have been heaped with reproach, because they do not recognize the "dreadful dilemma" into which they have put themselves by making conversion and salvation dependent on divine grace alone and not on human conduct also. But that which in the controversy, *inter disputandum*, was made, and is still made, the object of harsh censure, is exactly the position which the censurists themselves, as Christians, assume before God, *coram judicio Dei, quando conscientia in tentationibus cum sua indignitate luctatur.* For the union of the Lutheran Church in America with reference to the doctrine of Conversion and Election nothing more is needed than to bring the teaching which men profess in public into harmony with that which, as Christians, they believe in their heart.

---

[59] So even Calvin, Instit. III, 24, 27. On the reversion of the Calvinists to the Lutheran doctrine of universal grace, in pastoral practice, cf. von Schéele, Symbolik, III, 55.

9

Position of the Old Dogmaticians

IX. The Position of the Old Dogmaticians.

Among the most disagreeable features of the recent controversy were the discussions regarding the doctrinal position of the old dogmaticians. The American representatives of *intuitu fidei* claimed that they were proclaiming the "very same" doctrine as the old dogmaticians; and this claim we contested. The discussions of this point were disagreeable, inasmuch as the general Lutheran public was hardly able to follow these historico-dogmatical disquisitions. On the position of the Lutheran dogmaticians in the doctrine of Conversion and Election an opinion is expressed again in the Norwegian Articles of Agreement, to this effect, that the "second form" of the doctrine of Election may be granted a place alongside of that form of the doctrine which is found in the Holy Scriptures and the Lutheran Confessions, however, only on condition that this second form be taught in the sense which Pontoppidan, Gerhard, Scriver, and others among the fathers who were teachers in our Church connected with this form. It is plain what the Norwegian Articles would have us understand in the sense of Pontoppidan, Gerhard, etc., to be. The intention clearly is to exclude all *synergism* from the second form, especially the errors rejected in Thesis 5a—d, *i. e.*, in particular, good "conduct of man" as a ground on which their conversion, salvation, and election can be explained. Thus the discussion of the position which the dogmaticians occupy with reference to the doctrine of Election and Conversion has been reopened. Is it not possible to attain unity of opinion among us regarding the dogmaticians?

To begin with, let us be reminded that a difference of opinion regarding the old, as also of more recent dogmaticians does not necessarily involve a disagreement in doctrine. If there had been at the bottom of our thirty years of controversy only a difference of understanding as to what the later dogmaticians of our Church teach, that strife would have been sheer folly, indeed: a crime against the Church. Also within the Missouri Synod there have always been differences of interpretation with regard to the teachings of the later dogmaticians. Walther and Wyneken differed in their views of the old dogmaticians. Again, Walther and his colleagues in the theological faculty were not always agreed on this point. The difference may be due to several causes. In the first place, not all men have had equal time and opportunity for research work in the great field of the writings of the old dogmaticians. In the second place, even where two or more possess equal knowledge of the field, something depends upon their personal inclinations, to give prominence either to the meritorious or to the faulty elements in the presentation which the dogmaticians have made of doctrine. This, again, may depend upon the degree in which the investigator feels himself personally indebted to the old theologians. Walther's real watchword was: "Back to Luther and the sixteenth century!" Nevertheless he cherished a warm affection also for the later dogmaticians, because he found them to differ from modern theologians by their adherence to the Scriptural principle. Walther's pupils remember that his first estimate of nearly every one of the older theologians was, that he was a "most excellent" man, of "stupendous learning." Only with evident reluctance did he *find fault* with any of them. Mentioning—to cite an instance—Musaeus' doctrine concerning an activity of man "in the progress (*in progressu*) of conversion," Walther would say: "I am sorry that Musaeus propounded this doctrine, and that his *Herr Schwiegersohn* (Baier) has copied it after him," By his cordial regard for the old dogmaticians Walther ever felt prompted to put the best construction possible on all that they had written.

His colleagues were not always able to adopt his point of view. But this did not in any way disturb our unanimity in doctrine. Neither ought agreement in understanding what the position of the old theologians is to be demanded now as essential for unity of doctrine.

However, in the Norwegian Articles of Agreement much stress is again laid on the position held by the dogmaticians in the doctrine of Election and Conversion, and new discussions of a historical nature have thereby been occasioned. For this reason we desire to restate our opinion regarding the position of the old dogmaticians. we believe that differences of opinion as regards the old dogmaticians can be removed if we turn our attention to the decisive points. The difference which first of all developed between the Missourians and the American representatives of *intuitu fidei* was this: Iowa, and later also Ohio and Dr. Schmidt, and his Norwegian adherents, stoutly maintained that there doctrine was "the very same" as that of the old dogmaticians. They complained of being treated unjustly if they were called errorists and the same judgement were not pronounced upon the old dogmaticians. On our part the admission was freely made that the draft of the doctrine by our adversaries, with the characteristic formula "in view of faith," was indeed the same in outward appearance as that of the dogmaticians. At the same time, we maintained that our opponents filled this outward form with a content essentially dissimilar. Which of us was right?

Let us make the central question of our inquiry that point which has been termed, also by the other side, that "cardinal point" of the whole controversy, to wit, the question concerning "man's conduct." As far back as 1872, Iowa had declared that this very point is the principal matter of the entire controversy: "Here lies the real, innermost difference between the Biblical and the predestinarian" ("Calvinistic" is meant) "doctrine. According to the former, man's eternal destiny *is rooted* in the personal, free *decision of man* for or against grace offered in Christ. He (God) permits it to depend upon man's decision, whether He will show mercy to a person, or harden him."[60] Just so Dr. Schmidt and Ohio, a decade later, declared their principal concern to

---

[60] *Monatshefte*, 1872, pp. 87 sq.

be that conversion and salvation be made to depend, not only on the grace of God, but also upon man's conduct. The evidence for this is submitted above, and need not be repeated here. Now apply this to the matter under consideration: What is the position of the old dogmaticians? Mark well: the question at issue is not whether the evil conduct of man is the cause of his *non-conversion* and damnation, but whether *conversion*, etc., depends upon some good or right conduct on the part of man. If the latter is taught by the later theologians, then they agree in the "cardinal point" with Ohio, Iowa, Dr. Schmidt, etc., and the "Germain" and "Norwegian Missourians" have erred in denying the agreement of their opponents with the later theologians. On the other hand, if the later theologians do not agree with Ohio, Iowa, etc., in the "cardinal point," then the latter have erred by claiming agreement with the old dogmaticians.

Now, what is the truth of the matter? We are persuaded that, in the essential point, Dr. Stellhorn, in 1872, when he was still a member of the Missouri Synod, maintained the correct position over against Iowa. For its doctrine that man's conversion, salvation, and election ultimately rest upon man's self-decision or conduct, Iowa claimed agreement with the Lutheran dogmaticians. Dr. Stellhorn conceded the well-nigh constant recurrence, among the dogmaticians, of such terms and phrases as: Election *intuitu fidei, ex praevisa fide*, and: faith a cause of election, though not a meritorious cause, or: while some suffer their natural resistance to be overcome, others reject salvation through willful resistance. Having admitted this, Dr. Stellhorn, however, continues: "Prof. F. proceeds as follows: 'Thus there occurs at this point a personal decision of man himself, and it is in the dissimilar conduct of man over against grace offered to him, and in his own personal decision, that the cause must be sought why some are lost and others are saved.' But if Prof. F. thinks that with this statement he is still expressing the sense of the old dogmaticians, I *am firmly convinced that he is mistaken*.[61] I do not believe that he is able to cite a single passage from any of our dogmaticians where they concede that the final decision rests with man, *i.e.*, that in the

---

[61] Italics our own.

act, or process, of conversion man is able to decide *for heaven also.*"[62] After quoting Hollazius, to the effect that man does not actively decide himself for conversion, but is passively determined by converting grace, Dr. Stellhorn continues: "All our old dogmaticians, to my knowledge, teach like Hollazius. They go quite a way with Prof. Frischel; they frequently employ exactly the same language; they appear to stand on the same basis with him, but when, from premises common to them and him, Prof. F. draws the last and, to our reason, entirely necessary conclusions, they part company with him. While he would consistently go further, they are intentionally and purposely inconsistent, because in this matter they regard being inconsistent as the only correct mode of procedure. I should think that Prof. F. himself would have to concede without reservation that the situation is all we have sketched it; in other words, that the opinion of Prof. F. and others is not the opinion of our old theologians, in spite of much consonance in terms and in spite of the fact that part of the way they keep him company."[63] Dr. Stellhorn is right. If by "old dogmaticians" are meant those theologians of the 17th and 18th century who opposed the synergism of Latermann and his followers, and who combated the school of Musaeus (Musaeus, Baier, and others), it must be conceded that they teach the opposite of what Iowa and, at the later day, Dr. Schmidt and Ohio have taught, when they reach the decisive point—human self-decision or conduct as an explanatory cause in the doctrines at issue.

True, there is, decidedly, a defect in the position of these dogmaticians as compared with the sixteenth century theologians and the Formula of Concord. The theologians of the sixteenth century and the Formula of Concord, when *comparing* those who will be saved with those who will be lost, and discussing the question why some are converted and finally saved rather than others, *at once* tell the plain truth. They declare without any circumlocution: Here we are face to face with a mystery which we cannot expect to see solved until in the life to come. Nothing is known, in this life, beyond these two points: Conversion and salvation are solely the effect of

---

[62] Italics our own.

[63] *Monatshefte*, 1872, pp. 346—348.

divine grace; non-conversion and perdition are the result solely of human guilt. This is the doctrine of the Strassburg Formula of Concord (1563); of Moerlin, Chemnitz, Selnecker, Kirchner, and others; of the Formula of Concord, and the Apology of the Book of Concord.[64] The later dogmaticians, on the other hand, when approaching this subject, begin, at first, to argue in a manner so as to attempt an explanation of the mystery. This tendency is inherent in the very formula *intuitu fidei*, though it should be conceded that the term was first employed in combating Huber's *universal* Election and the Reformed *exclusion of faith from Election.* The same tendency, in many respects, is seen in the distinctions of various kinds of resistance and in the minute divisions of "prevenient grace." However at the critical point they do not say: "Hence the reason why some are saved and others lost is to be found in the dissimilar conduct of man over against proffered grace, in his personal decision," but at the end they desist from all explanations, and caution their readers to rest the whole matter with the statement of these truths: "Those who are converted and saved owe this to the grace of God alone; those who remain unconverted and are lost have themselves to blame." Gerhard writes: "With reference to the fact that many are converted and finally saved, it must be acknowledged that this is the work of divine grace alone; with reference to the non-conversion and damnation of others, it must be acknowledged that this is due solely to the guilt of those who are lost. With these simple, God-fearing statements the Christian may rest his mind securely, even if he cannot solve all difficulties which present themselves in regard to the individual persons who are to be converted."[65] Again, Gerhard says: "Hence the doctrine stands that conversion and perseverance depend upon the grace of the Holy Spirit alone; on the other hand, the cause why some are either not converted at all, or lapse from the grace of conversion, lies

---

[64]

[65] *Loci*; L. de libero arbitrio, § 57: Quod multi convertuntur et salvantur, agnoscendum est solis divinae gratiae opus esse; quod multi non convertuntur et pereunt, agnoscendum est ipsorum pereuntium culpa unice fieri, in qua pia simplicitate mens Christiana secure acquiescere posset, si vel maxime omnibus difficultatibus, praesertim iis, quae circa individua hominum convertendorum moventur, sese non possit expedire.

in the wickedness of man, which hinders and disturbs the work of the Holy Spirit."[66] Agreeably with the foregoing, Gerhard appropriates the words of Augustine on the *discretio personarum*: "What is now hidden from us will then (in the life everlasting) be manifest. Then the reason will be manifest why one was elected, the other rejected."[67] A particularly instructive remark, which shows the position of the dogmaticians, is found in John Musaeus. Musaeus, like Baier, assumed that there is a spiritual activity in man by means of powers imparted by grace *before* conversion, and he became involved in a controversy with Quenstedt and Calovius. But Musaeus renders a historically correct account of the Lutheran position. Wendelin, a Reformed theologian, had charged the Lutherans with locating *in man* the reason for the difference why some are converted, and others not. Musaeus replied: "Wendelin is not quite fair in presenting our teaching, and purposely quotes it in equivocal terms, in order to find fault with it. In the first place, our theologians are *not* accustomed to say that the reason for the difference why some are converted and others not, is found solely in man, but *all* say, *unanimously*, that the reason why those are converted who actually are converted is not found in man, but solely in God, and that the reason why those are not converted who remain in wickedness is not to be sought in God, but solely in man."[68] Thus we have here, at the decisive point, a difference equal to yea and nay between the dogmaticians and the American representatives of *intuitu fidei*. The latter refer salvation and perdition to a *common source*, the conduct of men. The former *divide the question*, and refer non-conversion and perdition solely and purely to man, and conversion and salvation to God alone.

---

[66] L. de elect., § 139: Manet proinde, quod conversio et perseverantia sint a solius Spiritus Sancti gratia; nihilominus, quod quidam vel non convertuntur vel conversionis gratia vicissim excidunt, ejus rei causa est in hominum contumacia, per quam opus Spiritus Sancti impediunt atque turbant.

[67] L. de vita aet. ., 74: Ibi quidquid nos nunc latet, manifestum erit; ibi ratio manifesta erit cur hic electus est et iste reprobatus, cur hic in regnum assumtus et ille in servitutem redactus.

[68] Collegium controversiarum, p. 390. Apud Baier, ed. by Walther, III, 227.

CONVERSION AND ELECTION

* * *

The quotations have been published in *Die Gruddifferenz,* etc., pp. 30 ff.: "In the *Strassburg Form of Concord*, of 1563, we read: 'However, why this grace, or this gift of faith, is not bestowed on all by God, while He calls all to Himself, and, accordingly to His infinite goodness, calls them with serious intent, this is a mystery that is hidden from us and known to God alone. It cannot be searched out by any man's reason, and must be reverently contemplated and worshiped, as is written: "O the depth of the riches both of the wisdom and knowledge of God! How unsearchable are His judgements, and His ways past finding out!" Rom. 11. And Christ thanks God the Father because He has hidden these things from the wise and prudent, and has revealed them unto babes, Matt. 11. Still we are not to become offended at these hidden ways of the divine will when we are troubled in conscience, but we must look at the will of God that has been revealed in Christ, who calls all sinners to Himself.' (See Loescher, *Hist. Mot.,* II, p. 288.)—*Joachim Moerlin*: 'It has been revealed to us that God will save only those who believe in Christ, and that unbelief is of our own doing. However, the judgements of God, *viz.,* why He converts Paul, but does not convert Caiaphas, why he restores fallen Peter while He leaves Judas to despair, are hidden from us.' (See Schluesselburg, *Catalogues Haereticorum,* V, p. 228.)— *Chemnitz*: 'What is the reason why Judas is not received, and does not obtain forgiveness of sin when he repents of what he has done? What is there lacking in his contrition and repentance that shuts him out from grace? He had not faith in Christ, he did not believe that God is gracious and forgives sin. That is the damaging fault in him. For where is there is no faith, there is no grace of God nor forgiveness of sin. Now, our Catechism says in the Third Article of our Christian Creed that no man can by his own reason or strength believe in Jesus Christ or come to Him, but the Holy Ghost must induce him to believe; for faith is a gift of God. How, then, does it come that God does not implant such faith in the heart of Judas, so as to enable him also to believe that Christ could help him? At this point we must turn back with our questioning and say (Rom. 11): "O the depth of the riches both of the wisdom and knowledge of God! How unsearchable are His judgements, and His ways past finding out!" We cannot and may not search out this matter, and we must not stray too far in such musings, but engage in all these matters in such a way as not to rush head-long into the sin of tempting God, lest God withdraw His hand from us and suffer us to sink and perish. For if we do this, we shall fall into sin upon sin, and shall gradually become merged in sin so deeply, that it is become impossible for us to return, and we cannot regain our former standing, as happened to Judas.' (*Sermons on the Lord's Passion,* IV, pp. 17 f.)—*Apology of the Book of Concord* (Chemnitz, Selnecker, Kirchner): 'Nor does the Christian Book of Concord deny that there is in God reprobation, or that God casts some away. Hence the Book of Concord does not go counter to the dictum of Luther, in his treatise *De Servo Arbitrio* against Erasmus, that this is the acme of faith, to believe that this same God who saves so few persons is nevertheless the most gracious God, and to be careful not to ascribe to God the real cause of such casting away and condemnation of men, which is the purport of the teaching of our adversaries, and to hold that, when this question is mooted, all men must put their finger on their lips, and, first, say with the Apostle Paul (Rom. 11): *Propter incredulitatem defracti sunt*; and, Rom. 6: "The wages of sin is death." In the second place, when this question is raised, why our Lord God does not convert all men by His Holy Spirit, and make them believers, which He could easily do, we must again say with the apostle: *Quam incomprehensibilia sunt judicia ejus et inpervestigabiles viae ejus!* But we must by no means charge God with having willfully and really caused the casting away and damnation of those who do not repent. However, if they urge this point, *viz.*: If you accept the choosing of the elect, you must also accept this other fact, *viz.*, that in God Himself there is from eternity a cause why men are cast away, even regardless of their sin, etc., we reply that we are in no wise minded to make God the cause of reprobation (which really has its origin, not in God, but in sin), nor shall we ascribe to God the real cause of the damnation of the wicked, but we shall take our stand on the saying of the Prophet Hosea, chap. 13, where God says: "O Israel, thou hast destroyed thyself; but in me is thine help." Nor shall we try—as we heard Luther saying above—to search out our heavenly Father as far as He is a hidden God and has not revealed Himself. For, though we try, the matter exceeds our ability, and we cannot comprehend it; the more we engage in such questioning, the further we get away from God, and the more we begin to doubt His gracious will regarding ourselves. Thus, the Book of Concord does not deny either that God does not operate in all men alike; for in all ages there have been many whom He did not call publicly through the office of the ministry. But our adversaries shall never succeed in convincing us that for this reason we must conclude, as they do, that God is the real cause of the casting away of these people, and that in His bare counsel He has decreed to reprobate and cast them away eternally, even regardless of sin. For when we approach this depth of the mysteries of God, it is sufficient if with the Apostle Paul in Rom. 11 we say: "His judgements are unsearchable," and, 1 Cor. 15: "Thanks be to God, which giveth us the victory through our Lord Jesus Christ." All that is beyond this will be revealed to us by our Savior Christ Himself in the life everlasting.' (*Apol. of the Book of Conc.* Dresden, 1584, fol. 206 f.) —*Selnecker*: "Though God could make willing all who are unwilling, yet He does not do this; and He has the most righteous and wise reasons why He does not do this, which reasons i does not behoove us to search out. We rather owe Him most cordial thanks because by the preaching of the Gospel He has called us to the communion of the life everlasting, and has enlightened our hearts by faith.' (*In omnes Epp. D. Pauli apost. Commentar.* Liepzig, 1595, fol. 213.)—*Timotheus Kirchner*: 'Since faith in Christ, now, is a special gift of God, why does He not bestow it on all? We reply: We should reserve the discussion of this question until the life eternal, and should meanwhile rest satisfied that God will not have us seek out His secret judgements (Rom. 11) : "O the depth of the riches both of the wisdom and knowledge of God! How unsearchable are His judgements!"' (*Enchiridion*, p. 143.)"

* * *

To proceed: What is the position of the dogmaticians as regards the notion of a *neutral state* before conversion? The assumption of a neutral state prior to conversion is always met with in connection with the doctrine that converting, saving grace is governed by the "self-decision" or "dissimilar conduct" of men. Whether "right conduct over against grace" is ascribed to natural powers or to powers imparted by grace, there is in each instance the supposition of a moment, or condition, *previous to* conversion, where man can "condut himself" or "decide" just as readily in favor of going to the right as to the left, just as readily in favor of heaven as of hell. During the controversy the assumption of a neutral condition of this kind was expressly demanded by Ohio. For example: "Accordingly, though the will of man has in no case any cooperative power, it is enabled to consent or to surrender. the point of time at which this power may be exercised is not discussed here. Certainly where no grace is offered, no consent can be given. But to him who hears the Gospel this grace is offered, and he may accept and surrender if he will, or he may resist if he will."[69] Just so Latermann in the seventeenth century: "We shall now prove that the grace of God is offered in such a manner that by virtue of proffered grace it lies within the power of man to perform by grace that which is necessary for conversion and salvation, or, if he yield to his depravity, not to perform it." "All can be converted *if they will*."[70] Now what do the dogmaticians say? They declare that it is "false and Pelagian" doctrine to assume that, owing to the operation of prevenient grace, there is in man a neutral state (*indifferentia ad utrumque oppositorum*) according to which man may accept or reject grace. In addition, they assert the non-existence of such a state.[71] We may sum up the position held by the dogmaticians over against Latermann and Musaeus, and their respective followers, somewhat like this: Conversion, in the strict or narrower sense,

---

[69] Lutheran Standard, August 19, 1882.

[70] Disp. de praed. thesis 32. 33. Apud Calov X, 24.

[71] *Quenstedt* II, 726: Bene monet Huelsemannus...falsum et pelagianum esse, quod in homine per gratiam praevenientem jam excitato et moto naturalis indifferentia ad utrumque oppositorum integra maneat, h. e. velle converti et non velle converti. Talis indifferentia in nullo homine reperitur... Indifferentia significat aequalem latitudinem ad libertatem potestatis, qualis neque in convertendo neque in converso existit.

consists in the bestowal of faith, and always takes place in a moment (*fit in instanti et in momento*). Death and life cannot exist together in man. There is no *status medius* between life and death. There are, indeed, in most cases, though not in all, certain motions called forth by the Word of God previous to conversion in the strict and narrower sense, *i. e.*, before the bestowal of faith. They term these motions "preparatory acts" (*actus praeparatorii*). But during these preparatory acts man is, and remains, *spiritually dead*; he is simply *subjectum convertendum*, the person that is to be converted. Man is not active in any of these *actus praeparatorii*. Also man's "passive conduct" previous to, and during, conversion is not an activity of man, but purely the work of God. Also in the matter of "passive conduct" man is merely passive. Calovius remarks that man's conversion takes place without the intention (*praeter intentionem*) and without the previous will (*praeter involuntatem*) of man.[72] Hence there is no moment of time and no state in which conversion *rests within the power of man*. The dogmaticians designate this as a *well-known* doctrine of "our theologians," *viz.*, "that a person's conversion is in no wise to be called free *in the sense that it rests with man's power* to will his own conversion."[73] They state again and again that whoever *wills* to be converted needs conversion no longer, being already converted. Nor do they think it proper to say that man desires conversion by means of *powers imparted by divine grace,* for "those powers are not conferred *previously*, in order that man may *afterward* be converted, through them, but the donation of spiritual powers is, as a matter of fact, conversion itself."[74] Quenstedt and Calovius specifically reject what they term an *error* in Musaeus, namely, that *motus spirituales*, "good motions, holy thoughts, pious desires," are ascribed to man before his conversion. For this rejection of good motions, holy thoughts, etc., before conversion they offer the following reason: "Wherever there are such

---

[72] *Systema*, X, 23.

[73] *Quenstedt* II, 726: Notae sunt nostrorum theologorum assertiones: Deum ex parte sua non tantum praestare, ut *possimus* velle, set etiam, ut *actu* velimus, nullo modo conversionem hominis eo modo liberam esse, ut in ejus potestate sit, *velle* se convertere.

[74] *Quenstedt* II, 727: Neque enim vires illae prius donantur, ut postea per eas homo convertatur, sed virium spiritualium donatio secundum rem est ipsa conversio.

motions, man is already quickened out of death, already lives in a spiritual life, and, consequently, is already converted."[75]

In framing his opinion of the dogmaticians, a person may easily be misled by scrutinizing a few expressions of ominous import and by ignoring the connection and added explanations. Quenstedt, for instance, speaking of "initial or prevenient grace" (*gratia incipiens* or *praeveniens*), says: "It declares the Word and, by means of it, the saving object, and thus removes (*aufert*) man's natural inability and unfitness in matters spiritual." This sounds exactly as if Quenstedt ascribed to man an inward spiritual change *before* conversion, which, according to Quenstedt's schema, takes place only when "operating grace" (*gratia operans*) has performed its work. However, while this expression is liable to be misunderstood,[76] we should do an injustice to Quenstedt if we were to impute to him the doctrine with the expression seems to involve. For a little farther down in the same chapter Quenstedt explains that after the removal of man's natural inability and unfitness there yet remains the natural and *actual* resistance, which is *utterly opposed* to spiritual things (*repugnantia spiritualibus prorsus contraria*). Hence, by the removal of natural disability through *gratia praeveniens,* Quenstedt does not understand an inner change *previous to* conversion, but merely this, that God *declares* unto man, who is still spiritually dead, His *Word*, which has the inherent power to convert; as he expressly says: "Prevenient grace leads man to the respective means of conversion and declares unto him who is still spiritually dead the Word, which has inherent converting power."[77] According to Quenstedt, spiritual life appears in man *after* the *gratia operans* and *perficiens*, which produces *faith*:

---

[75] *Quenstedt* II, 729: Certe ubi tales motus (that is to say, boni motus, sancta cogitatio, pium desiderium) sunt, homo est excitatus a morte et jam vivit vita spirituali et per consequens est conversus.

[76] The expression is adopted from Chemnitz's Loci. Just so Chemnitz in his Examen, p. 120: Tradit Scriptura, quod Spiritus S. in illis, quos vult convertere, primum incipiat pravitatem illam quam quoad motus et actiones spirituales in mente et voluntate non-renata invenit, mortificare et auferre, deinde incipiat operari et donare novam vim, facultatem et efficaciam in mente, voluntate et corde ad inchoandas et efficiendas actiones spirituales.

[77] *Systema*, II, 709.

*Gratia inhabitans fidem **subsequitur***, indewelling grace *follows* upon faith.[78] The dogmaticians never cease reminding Latermann and his followers that, if a willing of that which is spiritually good is ascribed to man *previous to* faith, the daughter is made older than the mother, since only faith *produces* a good will (*siquidem fides bonae voluntatis genetrix sit*).[79] When the Latermannians objected that an *irrisistible grace* and forcible conversion is taught, unless a neutrality or self-decision for conversion is assumed previous to conversion, they replied: "Irresistible grace is sufficiently repudiated by a reference to those who do *not* become converted; it is not necessary at all to assume a desire for grace before conversion in those who are to be converted."[80]

We would sum up our opinion of the seventeenth century dogmaticians who opposed Latermann and Musaeus, thus: The divisions of grace, as found in *Quenstedt*, for instance, are apt to cause confusion. Also *Chemnitz* would have done better, we believe, if he had reduced at least by two the five degrees (*gradus*) of grace which he quotes with approval from Augustine.[81] But Chemnitz retains the *sola gratia*, and the dogmaticians, spite of unnecessary divisions and digressions, arrive also at the conclusion: There is before conversion no neutral state in which man, by virtue of natural or grace-imparted powers, may conduct himself rightly over against grace, obtain free scope of action in the matter of his conversion and salvation, and may choose heaven as well as he chooses hell.

The difference between the American representatives of *intuitu fidei* and the dogmaticians is evident from the following juxtaposition:

Placing these and other expressions alongside of one another, we cannot but acknowledge this fact, *viz.*: In spite of the identical expression "in view of

---

[78] *Systema*, II, 713.

[79] Calov, *Systema*, X, 108; Joh. Adam Osiander, Colleg. th., IV, 322 sq.

[80] Staussburg Faculty, apud Calov, X, 54: Satis est, ut gratia non inevitabiliter determinet, si sit in potestate hominis ita pravitati suae indulgere, ut gratia divina excitante ad praestationem eorum, quae ad conversionem necessaria sunt, nolit, non opus est, ut in ejus potestate sit etiam velle. Neque sequitur si nolle sit in potestate et arbitrio hominis, etiam velle esse in ejusdem facultate.

[81] *Loci*; locus de libero arbitrio, c. VI, p. m. 473-487.

faith," etc., we have before us two doctrinal positions radically different, one occupied by the American representatives of *intuitu fidei*, the other by the "old dogmaticians." They have certain phrases in common, and a certain distance they travel the same road; but when they arrive at the critical point, the dogmaticians permit conversion and salvation to rest with God's grace, and hence teach also the certainty of salvation and election, while the American representatives of *intuitu fidei* draw the conclusions resulting from this "misleading expression," and base conversion and salvation, as far as the final issue is concerned, not on divine grace alone, but on human conduct, and consequently deny the certainty of salvation and election. An honest partition of the seventeenth century theologians would place Latermann, Dreier, Hornejus, and others, on the side of the American representatives of *intuitu fidei*, while Calovius, J. A. Osiander, and the theological faculties of the seventeenth century which opposed Latermann and his associates belong on our side.

The above inquiry is occupied principally with the doctrine of Conversion. It was in this doctrine that the real difference in the controversy lay. After some hesitancy this was admitted also by the other party. One's position in the doctrine of conversion determines the real meaning which one connects with the term *intuitu fidei*. Not that this "form" of the doctrine ever become *scriptural*. Not even by avoiding the admixture of synergism in the origin of faith. The second form, also minus synergism, is and remains contrary to the Scriptures, because it is contrary to all statements of Holy Writ that describe the relationship of the faith of the elect to their eternal election. The second form does not represent faith as an element in eternal election, but as an *antecedent* of election. Hence it does not represent the faith possessed by the elect in this life as a *product* and *result* of their eternal election, but represents the elect as having, according to divine foreknowledge, *accomplished* faith and the Christian estate before their election is put in operation. The contradiction to Scripture herein implied, and the impropriety of citing the προγινώσκην of Rom. 8, 26 in support of this position, we have again pointed out last year in *Lehre und Wehre*.[82]

***

L. u. W. 1912, pp. 196 ff.: "Scripture and the Confessions are also quite clare and unmistakable in what they say regarding the relation which the faith of the children of God *here in time* holds to their election in eternity. In all passages which treat of this relation the faith of the children of God and their entire state of grace is represented as a *consequence* and an *effect* of their eternal election. Scripture names as a consequence and an effect of eternal election the entire spiritual blessing which has been imparted to Christians here in time, Eph. 1, 3 ff., their calling, justification, and glorification, Rom. 8, 28—30, their being taken out of the world which is perishing (conversion), and their being placed in safety in the state of salvation, 2 Tim. 1, 9, their becoming believers, Acts 13, 48. Yea, according to Scripture it is a consequence and an effect of the election of grace that there exists at all in this world a Church, a communion of believers, and that, even in times of the greatest defection, such as the days of the Prophet Elijah, the days of the Apostle Paul among the Jewish nation, and the times of falling away prior to the day of Judgement, Rom. 11, 5; Matt. 24, 22—24. Could the Scriptures have stated with greater distinctness that faith and perseverance in faith are not an *antecedent*, but a *result* and *effect* of the eternal election? Likewise our Lutheran Confessions state in the oft-quoted words: 'The eternal election of God not only foresees and foreknows the salvation of the elect, but is also, from the gracious will and pleasure of God in Christ Jesus, a cause which procures, works, helps, and promotes what pertains thereto; upon this [divine predestination] also our salvation is so founded that "the gates of hell cannot prevail against it" (Matt. 16, 18). For it is written (John 10, 28): "Neither shall any man pluck my sheep out of my hand." And again (Acts 13, 48): "And as many as were ordained unto eternal life believed."' (Mueller, p. 705, § 8. Jacobs, p. 651.) Accordingly, this entire scheme of an election *intuitu fidei finalis*,

---

[82]

which makes faith and perseverance in faith an antecedent of the eternal election, is contrary to Scripture and the Confessions. Those Lutherans who want to retain this scheme must go to the trouble of *giving a different interpretation* to all the passages of Scripture which treat of election.—A proof from Scripture for the teaching of an election *intuitu fidei finalis* has been attempted. The statement (οὓς προέγνω), 'whom He did foreknow,' in Rom. 8, 29, has been cited. But these words are not suffered to express what they state in their literal meaning, but the interpreters take the liberty of casting aside the object 'whom' (οὓς), and substituting for it as object an entirely different concept: 'whose *persevering faith* He did foreknow.' Over and against this view Luther and our Confessions quite correctly understand (προέγνω) in this passage to describe *the act of 'electing' or 'foreknowing' proper*. That there is in God a 'knowing' of this kind which is synonymous with 'electing' is established beyond a doubt from such passages as Amos 3, 2: 'You only have I known of all the families of the earth' (; likewise Gal. 4, 9; Ps. 1, 6, etc.). Hence Luther adhered to Scripture when he rendered Rom. 8, 29: 'whom He did foreknow' (*versehen*), and did not take the liberty of inserting the gloss: 'whose persevering faith He did recognize or know before.' The Confessions, too, have adhered to Scripture when paraphrasing the passage Rom. 8, 29. 30, thus: 'Whom God did foreknow, elect, and ordain, them He also called.' Briefly, there is *no proof from Scripture* for the teaching of *intuitu fidei*. Those who teach this doctrine must do so *without*, and *contrary to*, the Scriptures. Likewise, violence must be done to the Confessions when the attempt is made to discover in them the teaching that faith is the *antecedent* of election. It is simply a fact, as appears from the statements above cited, that the Confessions do not place faith *before* election, as its antecedent, but they place faith and perseverance of faith *into* the very center of the eternal election, by declaring that *in* His eternal election God has ordained in what manner He would lead each Christian to conversion, righteousness, and salvation, and would preserve them therein. (Mueller, p. 714, §§ 44—47. Jacobs, p. 657.) The Confessions, moreover, represent the faith of the elect here in time, and their entire state of grace here in time, as a result and effect of their eternal election, by declaring that the eternal election of God from the gracious will and pleasure of God in Christ Jesus, is a *cause* which procures, works, helps, and promotes out salvation, and what pertains thereto. (Mueller, p. 705, § 8. Jacobs, p. 651.) For the purpose of evading these clear statements of the Confessions which are contrary to the teaching of *intuitu fidei,* an attempt has been made to ascribe to the Confessions the teaching of an election 'in a wider sense,' an election which comprises all men. But the Confessions utter a loud protest against this election 'in a wider sense.' At the very start they declare distinctly that they are speaking of an eternal election which 'pertains *not* at the same time to the godly and the wicked, but *only to the children of God.*' (Mueller, p. 705, § 5. Jacobs, p. 650.) Such are the difficulties which arise when men are not in harmony with the Scriptures and Confessions in the doctrine of election, but try to stick to the notion of faith and perseverance in faith as an antecedent of the eternal election. Assuming that both parties to the controversy accept the Scriptures and the Confessions, how much easier is it to let go of the idea of faith as an antecedent of election, and to reach agreement by allowing words of Scripture and the Confessions to stand, and by accepting them as they read."

* * *

It is, however, true that those teaching an election in view of faith, while regarding the actual issuance of faith as dependent upon man's self-decision or good conduct, employ the *intuitu fidei* in a sense quite different from the sense in which it is employed by others, who, while using this phraseology, still regard faith as a *donum Dei,* utterly independent of all human cooperation through "self-decision," "right conduct," "cessation of willful resistance," etc. In the latter event, God takes into consideration something He Himself *does*; in the former, God takes into consideration something *man* does. Accordingly, the dogmaticisans who used the expression *intuitu fidei,* but over against Melanchthon, Latermann, and others, rejected self-decision, neutrality, and the good conduct of man in conversion, fairly *implored* their readers not to imagine that in election a cause of the *difference* must be sought in man. Seb.

Schmidt: "In the predestined person there is as little cause of predestination as in the rejected."[83] Even Musaeus, as pointed out above, characterizes it as a slander upon Lutheran dogmaticians if any one attributed to them the teaching that they placed *the cause of the difference* why some are converted, and others not, in man. The American representatives of *intuitu fidei*, on the other hand, issue the imperial demand: The explanation of the difference that some are converted and finally saved, and others not, must be sought in the dissimilar conduct of men. "Hence the dissimilar operation of converting, saving grace may be explained by the dissimilar conduct of men over against grace."[84]

As to the *practical application* of the different views concerning Election, the following situation develops: Whoever has received the "first form" of the doctrine of Election into his heart, *i. e.*, whoever accepts the Scriptural teaching with regard to Election, thinks of his *redemption, call, justification, sanctification, and preservation* whenever his mind reverys to his election; and because all this is revealed, offered, and imparted to him in the *Gospel*, and believing on the Gospel, his election becomes evident and certain to him. Whoever has received the "second form" minus synergism into his heart, *i. e.*, whoever believes that God has foreordained men in view of persevering faith, will first of all look for that persevering faith which God had foreseen in him. It will not be long before he realizes that he does not and cannot know what God has foreseen in him. But because he retains the truth that God alone works and preserves faith, by grace in Christ through the Gospel, he no longer concerns himself about divine foreknowledge, but relies with heart, mind, and thought on the Gospel. Hence, because he holds fast *sola gratia* and the means of grace, his course of procedure ultimately coincides with the course implied in the "first form" of doctrine. Hence, too, the result is the same: certainty of salvation and election. Hence, the doctrine of the certainty of election and salvation is found in the writings of the anti-synergistic theologians of the

---

[83] *Aphorismi theol.*, p. 295: In homine praedestinato tam nulla est praedestinationis quam in reprobo causa.

[84] *Zeitblaetter*, 1911, p.526.

seventeenth century no less than in those of Luther and the theologians of the sixteenth century. But whoever has received the second form of doctrine *plus* synergism into his heart, *i. e.*, whoever believes that God has foreordained in view of faith, but makes faith and perseverance in faith dependent, not on the grace of God and the means of grace, but, in the last analysis, on man's good conduct, —such a person will turn away his heart, mind, and thought from divine grace and the Gospel, and will rely for the actual issue of his salvation upon his good conduct. And since he cannot know whether he will rightly conduct himself *"eventualiter, i. e.,* with reference to the final issue," he must, naturally, be and remain uncertain of his election. From this it will be manifest that in spite of the common phrase *intuitu fidei* there must be recorded an essential difference between the American representatives of *intuitu fidei* and the seventeenth century dogmaticians. At the same time it becomes quite plain how these latter, owing to their retention of *sola gratia*, are practically forced away from the incorrect formula "in view of faith," and were guided back to our standpoint, which is the standpoint of Scripture and the Lutheran Confessions.

In this connection we shall have to take up for a brief discussion Walther's statements of opinion of the dogmaticians. In the discussions to which the Norwegian Theses of Agreement have given rise, these statements of Walther were liberally quoted. Some have given their full approval to these statements as they understood them. Others, again, declared that in Walther's statements of opinion, contradictions must be recognized. We would observe, to begin with, that no serious fault should be found with a man for pronouncing variant opinions, in the course of time, and under the influence of variant impressions. Some one has said that it is unfair to expect of a man that he will never contradict himself. We do not enter as yet upon a discussion of Walther's position in the doctrine of Election. Whether there must be recorded a change in Walther's doctrinal position, is a question which will be taken up for brief treatment in Chapter XIV. We are interested at this point in Walther's utterances regarding the anti-synergistic dogmaticians of the seventeenth century. It seems to us that these utterances may be classified in two groups. On the one hand, Walther remarks that the dogmaticians who have employed the term *intuitu fidei*, have attempted a "development of doctrine" (*Lehrfortbildung*), introduced an "innovation," used a "misleading expression," which, "strictly considered," contains an "error" which the dogmaticians themselves condemn, the error, to wit, that there is a cause of election *in man*. Besides, he says that the dogmaticians have perverted the Scripture passages treating of Election by their attempt to force the *intuitu fidei* upon these texts, so that these men, otherwise so sure and powerful in the Scriptures, are hardly recognizable as the same men when they draw such "inconsequential conclusions" in the doctrine of Predestination. Moreover, Walther declares that these theologians have greatly injured the Lutheran cause in the controversy with the Calvinists through this introduction of the *intuitu fidei* formula, and that they have given the synergists a shelter where there error could hide. For this reason he declares: We believe that "we may best avoid misunderstandings, so easily called forth, if we entirely abstain from using the new terminology of the seventeenth century dogmaticians."[85] He considered the advisability of "entirely abolishing and no longer tolerating the expression 'in view of faith,' because modern synergists hide their error in this term."[86] This is one group of utterances. Alongside of these there is found in Walther's writings another group of opinions which do not only pronounce "our best dogmaticians"—he means the anti-synergistic theologians—to be "no errorists," but also declare that these men have essentially held fast the truth and defended it against the Calvinists. In pronouncing this opinion, Walther, first of all, acts upon the assumption that these dogmaticians have retained the *sola gratia* and have, by so doing, *themselves*, rejected the error involved in *intuitu fidei*. He finds that they "create the impression, in some passages, of leaning towards synergistic views of Election, but in other, much more numerous instances they correct themselves, and reject and condemn even the most subtle and hidden synergism."[87] As evidence he adduces from the dogmaticians such utterances as these: No converted person differs from,

---

[85] L. u. W. 1872, p. 140.

[86] Beleuchtung, p. 16.

[87] L. u. W. 1881, pp. 291 sqq.

nor can indulge boastfulness over and against, a non-converted person; in a predestined person there is as little cause of predestination as in a rejected one; in man there is no cause of the difference why some are converted, others not; cessation of willful resistance, so-called, is a work of God to which man can only offer resistance. According to Walther, *sola gratia* occupies so central a position in Christian doctrine that under its influence *intuitu fidei* is reduced to a mere formula. We have in the foregoing shown the soundness of this view by exhibiting the *practical application* of the variant views concerning Election. Whoever retains the "By-grace-alone" with reference to the origin and preservation of faith, and also the correct doctrine of the means of grace, will sacrifice the *intuitus* and cling to the Gospel, thus actually passing over to the first form and practicing it. Again, a complete surrender of the *intuitu fidei* is seen to occur whenever our dogmaticians teach the certainty of salvation and election. A "foreordination of grace" determined by the foreknowledge of God is an utterly unknowable matter, because no man, nor any Christian, is able, to know what God has foreseen. Inasmuch as our dogmaticians most certainly teach the certainty of election and salvation based upon the divine promises of grace, which make our salvation a matter to be disposed of by the Lord's hand and not by our own, they have, quite as certainly, in effect *forgotten the intuitu fidei* theory, have forgotten it not only in part, but wholly.

Besides this retention of *sola gratia* on the part of the dogmaticians, and the resultant corrective influence which sterilizes their theoretical malformations, another consideration influenced Walther towards a relatively favorable opinion of the dogmaticians. He inquires into their *intention*, he asks: What purpose did the dogmaticians have in view by using the term *intuitu fidei*? What *contrary view* did they seek to exclude? In his *Examen*, as well as in his *Loci*, Chemnitz remarks that in their efforts to reject error the church-fathers sometimes were led to say a great deal more than they intended (*gloriosius aliquanto locuti sunt*).[88] The *intuitu fidei*, as used by the dogmaticians, is a case in point. Samuel Huber demanded an election which would include all mankind, and insisted that all who did not accept this view

---

[88] Loci; Locus de viribus humanis, p. m. 436.

of a universal Election were Calvinists. Now since the Scriptures teach that the number of the elect is small compared with the number of those who are lost, and that only the elect are saved, the theologians were led, especially by the example of Aegidius Hunnius, to use the expression that God has foreordained men "in view of faith." But because they realized how very easily the expression might be misconstrued, as if it rested with man whether he should believe, thereby establishing a cause of election in man, they add a long series of *explanations* in order to exclude this meaning of the term. "Hence," they say, "we reject as wrong and wicked if any would say or teach that the believers elect God by faith before God elects them, or that they give Him a reason why He should elect them...On the contrary, faith comes originally from the eternal foreordination of God, and is not produced by us, but solely by the grace of God in us." They say: We are "elected unto eternal life by God, not for the sake of faith, but *through* and *in* faith, as St. Paul writes to the Thessalonians: 'God has chosen you from the beginning unto salvation in the sanctification of the Spirit and belief of the truth.'" Having cited these and other explanations of the *intuitu fidei* from the *Wittenberger Konsilien*,[89] he gives his opinion of these *intuitu fidei* theologians as follows: "Accordingly, all that these theologians endeavored to save, over against Huber, by means of their *intuitu fidei*, amounts to this: a *faith-less person, i. e.,* one who dies without faith, cannot be, or have been, an elect."[90] The explanations given by the theologians of a somewhat later date follow the same general line of thought, though there is an even more pronounced opposition to the Calvinistic conception of Election, which views the merits of Christ and faith not as an element in the eternal election itself, but merely as the execution of a foreordination once absolutely decreed.[91] Like Aegidius Hunnis and his contemporaries, they make a twofold observation. First, in the use of the

---

[89] I, 651 sq. 569 sq. 589 sq. 604. 609.

[90] L. u. W. 1880, p. 263.

[91] *Gerhard*: Non negatur Deum ex mera gratia salvandos ad finem et media praedestinasse, sed in eo consistit nervus controversiae, an Deus *primo* absolute quodam beneplacito ad finem quosdam praedestinaverit, quibis absolute electis *demum* constituerit dare media et per illa ad finem eos deducere. (De elect., 175.)

term "in view of faith," faith must not be understood as a prompting cause, as a condition to be fulfilled, as something good in man, which prompted God to foreordain the elect before others; and to prove this, they argued that faith is not something which rests with man, but is purely the work of God.[92] Secondly, they explain their purpose in using this term; they would merely emphasize the truth that faith *belongs into* the order of election and is not—in the manner of the Calvinists—*to be excluded* from election. Foreseen faith is really to be regarded not as a previous *condition*, but only as *a part of* the divine

---

[92] *Gerhard (L. de electione*, 161): "With a loud voice (*sonora voce*) we confess that we hold that God has found nothing good (*nihil boni*) in the persons whom He would predestinate to eternal life; that He had taken into account neither good works nor the use of free will, nor even faith in such manner that He was thereby prompted or for the sake of it had chosen certain persons; but we say that God had taken into account solely the merits of Christ, and has out of pure grace formed His purpose of election." Gerhard replies to the Calvinistic objection, that the Lutherans must assume a cause of *election* in man, it they put the cause of *reprobation* in man as follows: "Though God, in His ordinary mode of procedure, does not convert those who do not hear the Word...blaspheme the Word and resist the Holy Ghost, it does not therefore follow that it rests with man whether he will be converted (*in homine situm esse*), since it is the work of the Holy Spirit, and not of human powers, if man is converted through hearing the Word." *Quenstedt* II, 25: "The prompting cause (of election) is partly an interior one (*interna*), partly external (*externa, scil. Meritum Christi*). The internal cause is the grace of God which is actuated by its own self alone, and excludes all merit of human works, or anything that can be called a deed or action, whether it be done by *the grace of God* or by means of natural human powers. For God has not chosen us according to our own works, but out of pure grace. Also *faith itself* does not belong here, if viewed as *a condition*, more or less worthy either in itself or by reason of a value which God has added unto faith by His grace (etiam fides ipsa huc non pertinet, si spectator tanquam *conditio*, magis vel minus digna, sive per se, sive ex aestimio per voluntatem Dei fidei superaddito), because nothing of this sort belongs into the decree of election as a cause which moved or prompted God towards forming such purpose, but all this must be ascribed to the pure and unadulterated grace of God...This is evident from Rom. 9:15-16: "I will have mercy on whom I will have mercy. So, then, it is not of him that willeth, nor of him that runneth, but of God that showeth mercy."

order of election.[93] *Fides ingreditur decretum electionis,* faith enters into the decree of election—this statement is accepted by all, even if they cannot quite agree in their definition of the relation which faith holds to election.[94] From this point of view Walther's opinion of those whom he considered the "best" of the old dogmaticians may be understood. There is, therefore, no necessity, we believe, for assuming a contradiction in judgement, when Walther, on the one hand, unreservedly condemns *intuitu fidei*, and, on the other hand, maintains that theologians who employed the term occupied a materially correct position in the doctrine of Election. The former position he takes when he views *intuitu fidei* in the abstract, as an unscriptural expression, a fiction of men, incorrect in itself, inviting error, and affording a hiding place to error. The latter position he takes when he views the theologians *in concreto* who employ a mistaken formula and suffer great hardship because of their employing it, but break down what is erroneous in the formula by clinging to *sola gratia*. A characteristic of Walther's theological disposition here asserts itself. Walther was disposed to recognize as orthodox not as few, but as many persons as possible. He is stern in passing judgement on people whom he beholds sacrificing *sola gratia*. But people who hold fast this central doctrine gain his cordial good will, and he is confident that this truth which they hold will lead them to put away their error. From this point of view Walther during the controversy regarded the American representatives of

---

[93] *Quenstedt* II, 53: Fides ingreditur electionem non ratione ejusdam dignitatis merioriae, sed respectu correlati sui, sive quatenus est unicum illud medium apprehendandi meritum Christi, sive fides non est causa meritoria electionis, sed dumtaxat conditio praerequisita seu potius pars ordinis divinitus in electione constituti. Electi sumus non διὰ τήν πίστιν, sed διὰ της πίστεως, non propter fidem, sed per fidem et in ea. Quamquam inter nos et Calvinianos hoc solum quarentur: utrum praevisa fides ad electionis negotium pertineat, hic disputare nihil prodest, cum illi fidem ad electionem attinere simpliciter negant. Walther adds the observation: "It is very remarkable how Quenstedy here corrects himself, by concluding, after a reference to other relations and bearings of faith upon election, with the remark that faith is rather part of the order established by God in election." (L. u. W. 1881, p. 104.)

[94] Gerhard: Non dicimus ex praevisione fidei esse praedestinationem, sed intuitum fidei ingredi electionis decretum, inter quas propositiones magna est differentia, prior causem meritoriam vel προχαταρχτικήν exprimit, posterior saltem ordinem denotat. (De elect. § 175.)

intuitu fidei as altogether different from the old dogmaticians who employed the same term. The latter he regarded, in spite of their false phraseology, as confessors of *sola gratia*. The former, who have drawn the consequences of this faulty expression, he regards as gainsayers of *sola gratia*, because they claim that the conversion, salvation, and election of men depends not on divine grace alone, but also on their own right conduct.[95]

We are under no obligation to judge of the dogmaticians as did Walther. But we are convinced that as a matter of fact the American and the old representatives of *intuitu fidei* do not belong in the same class. In one respect it would have been easier for us during the controversy if we had made the *intuitu fidei* the "broad ditch" separating warring factions, and if we had placed all those who said *"intuitu fidei"* on yonder side. We for our part were able to dispense with the later dogmaticians. As it was, we have ample consensus on our side. We have the consensus of Scripture, the consensus of Luther and the sixteenth century theologians, the consensus of our Lutheran Confessions. That is consensus enough. Why go to the trouble of citing authority to prove that the later dogmaticians use the term *intuitu fidei*, like our opponents, but connect a different meaning with the term? We confess—we have occasionally been inclined to spare ourselves the trouble. We have noticed similar feelings in Walther. But we should have given he lie to history if we had yielded our assent to the claim of the other party, that it taught *"the very same"* doctrine as the old dogmaticians. Besides, what would have become of the justice of

---

[95] Walther: "It is quite unnecessary to argue separately on the 'in-view-of-faith' or on the general relation of faith to election, because whenever our opponents speak of 'in-view-of-faith' they do not really, like the best of our dogmaticians, mean faith, but, like all thoroughgoing synergists, always man's 'conduct.' We might in a way tolerate the 'in-view-of-faith,' because it is susceptible of a favorable interpretation; but 'in-view-of-man's-conduct' permits of no favorable interpretation, but is rawest sunergistic Pelagianism, which entirely precludes correct teaching with regard to penitence, conversion, faith, salvation by grace, etc. Synergistic Pelagianism perverts and destroys all this fundamentally, and brings into the Church a new, un-Christian, unevangelical doctrine of the way of salvation. It is the doctrine of the so-called scholastics, of whom Luther wrote: 'The sophists were accustomed to say: If man does his share, or as much as he is able, God surely will not fail to give him His grace.': (Berichtigung, pp. 149 sq.)

a theologians's opinion if we had classified those who *reject* self-decision, neutrality, good conduct, with those who *defend* the same as a reason for explaining conversion and salvation?

However, the relatively favorable judgement which we are compelled to pass upon the old dogmaticians as compared with the American representatives of *intuitu fidei* must not induce the American Lutheran Church to concede to *intuitu fidei* equal rights within the Church with the doctrine of Scripture and of the Confessions. There is a difference between excusing a faulty expression in persons who explain it better than the words import, and to concede to the faulty expression equal rights with the correct expression. Inasmuch as the "second form" verily does contradict Scripture and the Scriptural confession of our Church, neither an individual person nor a number of persons, nor a Synod, nor several Synods, nor the entire Church has authority to sanction its use within the Church. The "second form" has never been of service to the Lutheran Church, but has been a source of much *harm*. The struggle for the Scriptural and confessional doctrine of Election within the American Lutheran Church would not have been so difficult and would not have caused so much division and sorrow if the advocates of the doctrine that converting, saving grace is governed by the right conduct of man, had not been able to find apparent cover behind the *intuitu fidei*. Nor did *intuitu fidei* ever aid the old dogmaticians in their struggle agains the false teaching of Calvinism on election, but has always harmed them. The Calvinists pointed out to them their departure from Luther and from the Lutheran Confessions, and also their perversions of Scripture texts treating of Election. As a matter of course, *nothing but* harm can ever result when those opposing false doctrine exceeded the proper limits on their part, and place themselves in contradiction with the Scriptures. The champions of false doctrine, in such event, seize the opportunity of persuading themselves and others that the defenders of correct doctrine are just as little to be relied upon in those matters which they teach correctly according to the Scriptures. The poor success of the dogmaticians in convincing Reformed church people of their Calvinistic error, is owing, in part, to the fact that the dogmaticians, on their part, mixed the anti-scriptural alloy of *intuitu fidei* with the doctrine of Election. It was not by the old dogmaticians, but by the Apology of the Book of Concord that the Calvinistic doctrine of Election was combatted on correct grounds.

Finally, too, it must be said that no Christian and no theologian as a Christian has ever had any *practical use* for the "second form," since, as repeatedly stated, the divine foreknowledge of *fides finalis* must remain an inscrutable divine mystery to every Christian. But—possibly *intuitu fidei* possesses some value to the "theologian?" During the controversy on predestination, some one—we do not remember who it was—expressed the sentiment that the "first form" is the best for the *Christian*, while the second is of service to the *theologian*. The latter is true only when the theologian does not regard "foreseen faith" as a gift of God, but teaches that converting, saving grace is governed by the dissimilar conduct of man. If, on the other hand, the theologian in harmony with Scripture and the Lutheran Confessions declares *that there is no such thing* as "dissimilar conduct," and that those who will be saved, *as compared with* those who will be lost, likewise conduct themselves ill over against grace and are in equal guilt, the theological advantage, too, is lost. For in that case we can discover absolutely nothing *in ourselves* by which God might have been governed in the matter of our conversion and election. In short, no theologian who really holds fast the *sola gratia* has ever explained aught by means of *intuitu fidei*. This applies to Gerhard, Scriver, Pontoppidan, Quenstedt, Calovius, Joh. Adam Osiander, and others. These precious men have caused much trouble to themselves and to others by means of *intuitu fidei*, and have partly dulled the edge of their sword against Calvinism, and yet have gained nothing from the viewpoint of the theologian. Therefore we say once more: the American Lutheran Church should not by any means yield to the *intuitu fidei* any right to exist alongside of the teaching of the Scriptures and the Confessions.

Hence, objection must be raised to the Norwegian Articles of Agreement, because they coordinate the "second form" with the first and recommend its adoption: "The Synod and United Church committes on Union acknowledge unanimously and without reservation the doctrine of Predestination which is stated in the Eleventh Article of the Formula of Concord (the so-called 'first form of the doctrine') and in Pontoppidan's Explanation (*Sandhed til Gudfrygtighed*), Qu. 548 (the so-called 'second form of the doctrine')." The rejection, in Thesis 5, of *synergism*, that prolific source of division and offense in the American Church, must be acknowledged to be a great achievement. All good Lutherans should acknowledge that this is a result of the union movement and something for which they should thank the Lord from all their hearts. This is a great forward step in the direction of true unity. The common *basis* has now been found from which efforts towards removing such uneven parts, as still remain in the Articles, may proceed. One of these is the coordination of the first and second forms of doctrine in Thesis 1. The matter, we know, stands thus: Only the first form is the form of the Scriptures and the Lutheran Confessions; the second form can only be traced to a number of teachers in the Church. Moreover, the second form must be interpreted at variance with its literal sense, in order not to be in contradiction with the doctrine of the first form. Besides, the fact has been recognized in the Norwegian Synod, and witness has been borne, not only to the effect that the second form has no ground in Scripture, but that it even invites error, and that it has at all times, and particularly in the recent controversy, afforded a shelter to synergism. "The second form"—to quote once more an excellent summing-up of the matter—" is *an attempt at finding a solution*; it is an attempt to solve a great difficulty, an attempt to render that comprehensible and reasonable which in our opinion must remain unsolved." "The *first* form of doctrine is very inconvenient for Semipelagians and Synergists; they can hide behind the *second* form, but not behind the first."[96] Accordingly, it should not require lengthy negotiations to agree on the elimination of the words in Thesis 1, which accept "without reservation" the second form together with the first. Nor should the predicament be lost sight of, into which simple Christians are brought through this very "second form." According to this form of doctrine, faith and the whole Christian estate are *antecedents* of their eternal election. Now, they read in their homes, or hear in church such texts as the following: 2 Tim. 1, 9: God "hath saved us, and called us with an holy

---

[96] *Dr. Stub* in *L. u. W.* 1881, pp. 473. 472.

calling not according to our works, but according to His own purpose and grace, which was given us in Christ Jesus before the world began," or Eph. 1, 3, sqq.: "Blessed be the God and Father of our Lord Jesus Christ, who hath blessed us with all spiritual blessings in heavenly places in Christ, according as He hath chosen us in Him before the foundation of the world, that we should be holy and without blame," etc., or Acts 13, 48: "And as many as were ordained unto eternal life, believed," or Rom. 8, 29: "Whom He did foreknow He also did predestinate to be conformed to the image of His Son. Moreover, whom He did predestinate, them He also called; and whom He called, them He also justified; and whom He justified, them He also glorified,"—as often as Christians read and hear such passages of Holy Writ, they recognize at once that their faith and Christian estate is not an antecedent, but a result and product of their eternal predestination. They must become confused and offended if they are asked to accept "without reservation" also the "second form."

On the other hand, it is proper to issue a warning, *viz.*, that in settling our relation to the old dogmaticians we must not reject the good with the bad. During the controversy regarding the Scriptural and confessional doctrine of Election, we have been constrained, more than at other times, to point out the *weak points* in the teaching of the seventeenth century theologians. And, indeed if we look about for *models*, in a theological way, we must turn not so much to the seventeenth century as to Luther and the sixteenth century. But it were a pity if we should no relegate to oblivion, as no longer worthy of our interest, the theologians of the seventeenth and early eighteenth century. Only recently we have again noted in the American Lutheran press recommendations, more or less fervent, of modern German theologians of the "positive" school. We foresee a danger to our Church if her students, from contempt of the old teachers of the Lutheran Church, confine their study to modern theological literature. These are the facts in the case: As yet there is more genuine theology, genuine with reference to contents and form, especially as regards the application of Scripture, to be found in *Hollazius*, and even in *Buddeus*, than in the best "positive" nineteenth century theologians of Germany. Hence, if American Lutheran theology were to substitute the positive theologians, so-called, of Germany as models of theology in the place of the old Lutheran teachers, it would be making a poor trade. We should, indeed, acknowledge an honest effort on the part of some german theologians, of late, to gain a firm footing in Christian doctrine in the midst of universal distraction and doubt. There is a manifest desire to return to Christian truth. Yea, these men would be "Lutheran." But for the time being they seem to be at a loss how to accomplish this. Even those at present regarded as the best, and who are, relatively considered, really the best among them, do not yet dare *to regard the Bible as the Word of God and to treat the objective Word of God as the only principle of theological knowledge.* By their denial of verbal inspiration—and there is no other kind of Scripture-inspiration—the whole order of things in theology still remains turned topsy-turvy in principle. When determining what is Christian doctrine, those theologians do not take their stand on Scripture as the deciding factor, but on their "experience," or on their human *ego*. This should not be overlooked by the American Lutheran Church.

But are the old Lutheran theologians not weak in *exegesis*? Especially in Germany there is frequent mention of the "dogmatical" exegesis of the old Lutheran theologians. It must be conceded that there are instances of "dogmatical" exegesis in the Lutheran dogmaticians. To use the language of Luther: they sometimes have right thoughts in the wrong place, *i. e.,* they cite certain texts in support of a doctrine which is not taught there, but elsewhere. The modern theologians, however, not excluding the positive, in spite of their vaunted "progress in exegesis," have, with rare exceptions, wrong thoughts in the right place. They are so completely dominated by their faulty dogmatics that they do not find Christian doctrine stated in the most lucid texts. We cannot but term this talk current fiction that is being circulated with no effort at verification, *viz.,* that the Lutheran dogmaticians were men who merely recorded dogmas according to the *traditional dogmatics*, and following the lead of the *Confessions*, and that they were little concerned about Scriptural evidences and the extraction of doctrine from the Scriptures. Whoever has taken the pains to study even superficially the great dogmaticians, such as Gerhard, Quenstedt, Calovinus, has had his opinion of these men changed completely, if he studied only so much as a single *locus*. With *Gerhard* the exhibition of doctrine from the Scriptures is the beginning, middle, and end of his effort. The texts quoted by the opponents are so exhaustively treated by Gerhard with reference to their context and linguistic usage that his treatise suffers more from over-penetration than from lack of penetration. *Quenstedt,* called the great "bookkeeper of Lutheran theology," presents mainly the *Scriptural evidence* in the notes under θεσις, as well as under βεβαίωσις, and ἐκδίκησις, in his great dogmatical work. *Calovius'* greatness as a Scriptural theologian is evident not only from his *Biblia Illustrata,* but from all his major works. Calovius it was, too, who never tired of recommending to students of theology the knowledge of Hebrew and Greek as much more necessary than the study of the fathers and the scholastics.[97] Meusel's *Lexikon* very aptly remarks on the fashionable disparagement of the old theologians as exegetes: "The adduction of evidence from the Scriptures has a prominent and extended space in old Lutheran dogmatics. Especially the authors of the *Loci,* and also of the later *Systemata,* are fully in earnest in regarding Scripture not merely as a touchstone for testing doctrines derived elsewhere, but as their *principle* and *source,* and derive from it the truths of dogma which they logically establish and defend against the objections of adversaries, so that the dogmatical writings of, *e. g.,* Chemnitz and John Gerhard are *a mine of thorough exegetical investigation.*"[98]

In connection with these utterances regarding the old dogmaticians, we may be privileged to say a few more words on *Dr. Walther's* theological manner. The association is not an accidental one. Especially in Germany, Walther has been grouped with the old Lutheran theologians. Even theologians who were in a way favorably inclined toward us classified Walther as a "theologian of reprisintation." They would call him the great "theologian of quotations," but in their estimation he did not pass as a "theologian of

---

[97] Calovius, *Theol. Antisyncretistica*, th. 4: Theologiae studioso longe magis necessaria est linguae hebraicae et graecae notitia quam theologiae scholasticae aut patrum stadium aut philosophiae.

[98] *Sub voce* "Schriftbeweis," VI, 93.

Scripture." He has gradually been brushed aside as not worthy of further consideration. This has resulted in a distinct loss to the Church in Germany. That theological method which his earlier associates, like Delitzsch, in their first ardor also espoused, but later deserted under the pressure of theological "science," reached complete *development* in Walther. When Count Erbach on an American tour became acquainted with Walther and with Walther's theological manner, he wrote: "Many years of fierce struggle for the truth, ceaseless labor and effort for the extension of the Gospel have developed in this man so adamantine a certainty and such luminous clearness in all matters of faith that I was lost in amazement and finally concluded: This is the man; God has chosen him for this country; He could not have found a better one. And in truth, He has, midst storms and tempests, employed this tool in rebuilding, on the rock of our Confession, His Church in the New World. Through him He founded a new home for the Lutheran Church…America is now the hope of Lutheranism. While elsewhere throughout the world there is heard the crash of the wreck and ruin of things, here the seed of truth undefiled is quietly and unwearyingly sown, cultivated, and watered by men who are undisturbed by the discordant noise of the world, armed with weapons of battle, ready at a moment's notice to rush to the defense. And the seed visibly brings forth fruit a hundred-fold…Not a grain of revealed truth is to be surrendered; rather let everything else perish! Such conditions are a source of comfort to all who are concerned about the future of the Church. With such armament the great, decisive battles may be fought without fear of the issue."[99] But even in the greater part of the American Lutheran Church—much to its damage—Walther has been pushed aside as not worthy of serious attention. The fiction that Walther was not really a "Bible theologian" has done its work here also. A fiction, we said. For this opinion, that Walther was not a "Bible theologian," can be reached only by one who measures Walther's books with a yardstick. We acknowledge that we, too, did this, though only for a short time. Rev. Hochstetter used to admit that his had been the same experience. If the yardstick is applied,

---

[99] E. A. W. Krauss, Lebensbilder, p. 727.

the result is, indeed, that in Walther's works citations are seen to occupy by far the greater amount of space. Closer acquaintance, however, develops the fact that this *"Zitatentheolog"* is through and through a *Schriftheolog*. Dr. Stoeckhardt, who presumably had some exegetical knowledge, in his last years repeatedly dwelt upon the impression which Walther's skillful manner of using the Scripture in *Kirche und Amt* made upon him when he was still in Germany. How does Walther go at his task in *Kirche und Amt*? He will cite the relevant texts of Scripture, and, by adding brief remarks, confine his effort to holding the reader to the clear texts of Scripture. By merely *underscoring* the decisive words in a text, he will sometimes attain the same end. When Walther desires to show from the Scriptures that God converts solely "by grace, for Christ's sake," and is not governed by perceiving "dissimilar conduct" in men, he quotes Rom. 3, 23. 24: "There is no difference; for all have sinned and come short of the glory of God; being justified freely by His grace through the redemption that is in Christ Jesus." Walther merely adds: "When the Holy Spirit here says that there is no difference among sinners, it follows that *in man* there can *never* be anything for the sake of which God converts *just him*, and not another." Every one must admit that in this manner the whole argument regarding the *discretio personarum* is definitely settled on the basis of Scripture. Again, when Walther desires to prove from the Scriptures that the Church in the real sense of the word consists exclusively of *believers*, he cites Eph. 1, 22. 23; 5, 23-27; 1 Cor. 3, 16. 17; Heb. 12, 23, and other texts, and simply *underscores* the words "Head of the Church, which is His body," "Church is subject to Christ," "glorious" ἔνδοξος, "not having spot or wrinkle," "holy," "without blemish," "the temple of God is holy, which temple ye are," "the Church of the first-born, which are written in heaven." Every one will concede that the truth: the Church consists only of the believers, is hereby exhibited and proved *from the Scriptures*. Walther is the theologian of the *bare* Scriptures (*nuda Scriptura*) i. e., of the scriptures without "gloss," or interpretation. This, and only this, affords an explanation of Walther's amazing certainty, which not only impressed Count Erbach, but was recognized as a characteristic of Walther by many outside of our own circles. Walther is also in this respect a true disciple of Luther. Luther bewails as the greatest affliction of his time the opinion that Scripture without exegesis, or "gloss," is *dark*; that the "interpretation of the fathers" was necessary for its understanding. Even while sojourning at the Wartburg, Luther called to the world and the Church: "No clearer book has been written on earth than the Holy Scriptures." "When a believer but hears the Scriptures, they are so clear and full of light to him that he says, *without any gloss of fathers and teachers*, 'That is true; that I believe.'" "But if someone were to approach you and say, 'We need the interpretation of the fathers, the Scriptures are dark,' you must say, 'That is not true.'" If they tell us that the Scriptures without the interpretation of the fathers is dark, their purpose is "to lead us out of the Scriptures, darken our faith, mount the nest, and sit on the eggs themselves and become our idols."[100] Elsewhere Luther expands on the matter: The *text* of Scripture is ever and unvariedly more clear than the exegesis or "gloss," because the correctness of the exegesis must ever be shown by reference to the text. Not only part of our doctrine, but the *whole* Christian doctrine is revealed in Scripture passages so clear that they stand in no need of a commentary. The obscure texts—for there are such—contain nothing that is not taught in the clear ones. By asserting that the clear texts, containing the whole of Christian doctrine, must, in turn, be made still clearer, the Scriptures are knocked into a confused, disjointed mass. If any would "teach" or "fight" with an interpretation, instead of the "nude" Scriptures, Luther designates the attempt an absurdity. If many readers and hearers find the clear Scriptures obscure, the cause must be sought in their ignorance, or limited knowledge, of the *language* of the Holy Writ. *Real* obscurities will not be made clear by the joint effort of all exegetes in the world. People may busy themselves with obscure passages for their entertainment, but not for the purpose of "teaching" or "disputing." Luther writes against Emser:[101] "The writings of all fathers should be read with humility, not to believe them, but to examine them whether they employ clear *texts*, and explain the Scripture by means of clear Scripture. How could they have overcome the heretics if they had fought

---

[100] St. L. Ed. V, 334 sq.

[101] St. L. Ed. XVIII, 1293 sq.

by the aid of their own *glosses*? If they had tried to do so, they would have been considered fools and beside themselves. But because they use clear *texts* that *need no gloss*, with such effect as to take captive every man's reason, the Evil Spirit with his heresies was forced to yield. There is another way of studying Scripture, which consists in expounding *obscure* passages and figures. This is a sort of huntsman's sport, and consists in hunting for, and finding, some merry interpretation, that is, one which affords delight, just as you hunt game. But that study which serves for spiritual *warfare* consists in *becoming versed in the Scripture*, as Paul says, mighty and richly supplied with clear texts, so as to be able to fight without any gloss or interpretation, as with a *naked drawn sword*, as was signified by the golden spears in the temple of Solomon, in order that the opponent, vanquished by the bright light, might see and confess that the texts are of *God* alone, and require no human interpretation." But if this is so, what need is there of that special grace of some teachers, the peculiar exegetical grace with which the Lord endows some, and in what way are we benefited by this gift? It is not required for making clear *the Scriptures*, but for *leading* the vagrant mind of man, who is a fugitive from the Bible, *into the clear texts* of Scripture, and to *hold him* to the *clear* Word, spite of all perverters of the same. In his introduction to Luther's explanation of John 17,[102] Harless made a remark on the relation of exegesis to the text of Scripture which reveals his correct understanding of Luther's exegetical principles. Harless wrote: "True, the Word itself has no need of human interpretation, yet our hard hearts and deaf ears require the voice of heralds and preachers in the desert. Nor are these necessary because the words of Christ were too high and too deep, too obscure and mysterious, for men's senses, but because we human beings, as Luther correctly says, in our perverse desire for false eminence, *pass unheedingly* over the divine simplicity of Christ's words, like blind men, or half-witted." These principles of Luther had passed into the very woof and warp of Walther's nature. We have ourselves heard him utter them with great enthusiasm in his hermeneutical lectures. Walther, like Luther, took his stand on *bare* Scriptures, and this explains, as noted above, Walther's

---

[102] Leipzig, 1857, p. V.

great assurance, so similar to Luther's. When the Colloquy at Marburg concerning the Lord's Supper was about to commence, Luther pushed aside the velvet table-cover, and wrote upon the table, not an *interpretation* of the words of institution, but these words *themselves—Hoc est corups meum*. The theologian, says Luther, must cling to the mere Word as a vine clings to the tree. Thus Walther, too, in spite of his many quotations from the old theologians, in his heart and conscience took his stand on the Word unmodified by interpretation. We have frequently heard him deplore the fact that he was unable to read the simple Scripture text as much as he liked, because of the stress of work. But at least the two hours before services every Sunday morning, he would devote to uninterrupted Bible reading, and would not permit them to be engrossed with any other task. We were reminded of Walther's attitude over against the Word by an utterance of his made during his last illness a month or two before he died. Looking back to the controversy on conversion and predestination, he said that if the Lord Christ would ask him on Judgement Day why he had taught as he did, he would say, Thou hast misled me in doing it, O Lord, by Thy Word. On the one hand, Walther declared it to be arrogance which God would punish, if, in getting doctrine out of the Scripture, a person refuses to be aided by others, or would not study the writings of the great teachers, but endeavored to find everything in Scripture himself.[103] On the other hand, he insisted that never an exegesis, but always the *naked* text, without exegesis, must be the determinative factor in the heart and conscience of the theologian. Such was Walther, the "theologian of repristination," the *"Zitatentheolog."* One may employ what is termed a heavy exegetical apparatus, and be admired as a great exegete by the unthinking masses, and et be anything rather than a "theologian of the Scriptural principle," a *"Schrifttheolog."* Compare *Walther* and *Franz Delitzsh*. The men were friends from their university days. Delitzsh has written a considerable number of commentaries, and is considered one of the greatest exegetes of all ages. Walther has not written a single commentary. His principal writings are amplifications of papers read at synodical meetings.

---

[103] See note to § 3 of his *Pastorale*.

Yet Walther is in the true sense of the term a "Bible theologian" because he has in every doctrine attained the sense of Scripture. Delitzsch, on the other hand, may only in a greatly modified sense of the term be called "*Schrifttheolog*," since he has not attained the sense of Scripture in such important doctrines as inspiration, creation, the person of Christ, the Church, and others, but has substituted his own opinions for the Scriptures. Similarly *von Hofmann*. In the ordinary church-lexica and theological encyclopedias he is called "one of the greatest Bible-scholars of all ages," who has worked "with pitiless philological exactness." Hofmann has written two volumes of *Prophecy and Fulfillment*, three volumes of *Scriptural Evidences*, an entire series of volumes inscribed, *The Holy Scripture of the New Testament Examined in Their Entirety*, and has lectured on Hermeneutics.[104] But was Hofmann a *Bible theologian?* Unfortunately *Kliefoth* is right when he characterizes von Hofmann's theology as follows: "A theological system which *does violence to the Scriptures*, disfiguring the doctrine of salvation by means of ingenious, but untrue combinations, and destroying the structure of Christian doctrine both by the admixture of philosophical elements to the more theoretical doctrines of God, the Trinity, creation, man, the person, natures, and states of Christ, and by weakening *throughout* the practical dogmas of sin, redemption, atonement, the work of grace, and the appropriation of salvation."[105] Kliefoth then mourns the fact that the exegetical and historical pretensions of von Hofmann threatened to work hopeless confusion, especially in the minds of the younger generation.

Everybody admits that doubt and confusion are rampant in the Churches of Germany. Whence this pitiful result after so much "progress of exegesis"? The mischief is much the same in our time as in the Reformation age: there is a disinclination to approach the Scriptures without "exegesis." Whoever confines himself, like Walther, to a presentation of the *mere* Scriptures, and to hold the reader or hearers to the *mere* Scriptures, is considered as lacking in exegetical training. According to this view, the Lord Jesus was exegetically

---

[104] Posthumously published by *Volck*. Noerdlingen, 1880. 7.

[105] *Kritik des Schriftbeweises von Hofmanns*. Schwerin, 1859, p. 559.

deficient, since in the temptation He quoted, over against Satan, the mere words of Scripture, without exegesis. And the Apostle Paul, of course, was entirely without exegetical proficiency, for did he not send a long epistle to the Roman congregation without adding an appendix in the shape of a much needed commentary? Modern theology, in its view of the clearness of Scripture, occupies essentially the *Roman Catholic* position. It regards as undue exaggeration the words of Luther: There is no clearer book on earth than the Scripture, and: Faith without exegesis understands the Scriptures if it but hears the words of Scripture. Some demand outright that the words of Luther concerning the clearness of Scripture must be "modified." Others accuse the Scriptures of obscurity at least in private conversation, and treat them accordingly. We American Lutherans, on the other hand, unreservedly subscribe to Luther's remark concerning the *clearness* of Scripture. Our efforts are directed in all our theological and exegetical work to the single end that hearers and readers may be led to the clear word of Scripture. On the "bare" Scripture we stand, with the "bare" Scripture we fight. From this point of view Dr. Stoeckhardt's splendid commentaries were written. True, this method of ours has won little approbation outside of our own circles, least of all among German theologians. Dr. Stoeckhardt's excellent commentaries have been simply ignored in Germany. It goes against the grain of modern theologians, as they are constituted, you know, to be remanded to the *bare* Scriptures and held down to the *bare* Scriptures. Not the word of Holy Writ, which is no longer regarded as the Word of God, but the *exegesis* is deemed of most importance, *i.e.*, in this instance, the human thoughts *superadded* to the Scriptures, furnish the materials for this theology. We American Lutherans are at pains to learn from any one who has something respectable to say. But in the matter of treating the Scriptures and Bible theology, foreign theology, in spite of its "exegetical progress," will have to learn from us. The arch-enemy of the Church has led Germany out of the Bible into the interpretation of the Bible. We, in America, have been led by the Holy Spirit from interpretation of the Bible into the Bible itself. We cannot suffer any to take from us the honor of being Bible theologians. Especially with regard to Walther we maintain that he was preeminently a "Bible theologian," according to Luther's definition:

"Whoever is well grounded and experienced in the text will become a good and efficient theologian; for one verse or text from the Bible counts for more than many authors and glosses."[106] An agreement in this truth and a squaring of action with the same would lead to the union, so devoutly to be desired, of the whole American Lutheran Church.

This discourse has imperceptibly grown beyond the intended length. But this point is of the very highest importance. *This is the point which separated us in the recent controversy*, and at this point unity must commence if it is to be established at all. In the recent controversy *Bible-text* and exegesis stood in opposition to each other. The other side insisted with much emphasis that the few Scripture-texts treating of Predestination were "obscure," and must needs be "interpreted" in order that universal grace might be preserved.[107] We on our part maintained that the texts treating of Election are sufficiently *numerous* and *clear*. Just so our Confessions: "Holy Scriptures not only in but one place and incidentally, but in many places, thoroughly discuss and urge the same" (doctrine of Election).[108] The texts concerning Predestination require, as little as the *sedes doctrinae* of other articles, an "interpretation" in the sense that obscure words must first be explained. What Luther says concerning Scripture texts for all Christian doctrine applies also to the texts which treat of Election: "When Faith only hears the Bible, it is so clear and bright to him that he says without any fathers and glosses: That is right, that I believe." We have, on occasion, requested the other side repeatedly to make the test. We have suggested that a Christian of average intelligence who knows nothing of the controversy be found in such passages as 2 Tim. 1, 9 or Eph. 1, 3 sqq. be read to him, with no interpretation added. The result would be that

---

[106] Erl. Ed. 57, 7.

[107] Dr. Stellhorn in "Worum handelt es sich," etc., p. 10: "And…this universal comfort of the Gospel can only be preserved if the few texts of Holy Writ, in part not easily understood, which treat of a selection of a few persons, who will infallibly be saved, are not interpreted in such a way that the many clear texts of the universal grace of God towards all men are darkened or suppressed, but if, on the contrary,…the few dark passages are interpreted by means of the many clear passages."

[108] Mueller, 704, § 2. Jacobs, p. 649.

the believer would recognize faith and the Christian estate not as an *antecedent* but as a *product* and *result* of eternal election. The texts dealing with Election are certainly clear enough. Nothing is needed beyond *believing* what has been clearly expressed. This fact has determined *our* exegetical method. Of course, we have also written quite a number of exegetical articles of varying length. But whoever will take the trouble to examine these articles will immediately admit that *our* whole exegesis consisted in simply directing the reader to the clear text of Scripture and *holding him to it.* Every means was exhausted in the effort to lead us away from the Scripture-text. We were reminded that the texts treating of Predestination must, of course, be interrupted agreeably to John 3, 16, or, at any rate, according to the scope of the entire Scriptures. Otherwise, it was said, we would be in a "dreadful predicament." Quite a series of titles was applied to us. We acted in accordance with a remark of Luther's, repeatedly quoted by us: "I will gladly suffer all vituperation, but will not yield one finger's breadth from the mouth of Him who says: 'Him ye shall hear.'"[109] When viewing the principle by which Christian doctrine is known, we are forced to say that the controversy most certainly revolved about this one question: "Bible-text" or "gloss"? As often as in the Church any controversy has arisen, this question was at bottom the controverted one. As Luther never tires of urging, the "gloss" started the mischief in paradise. The words: "Of every tree of the garden thou mayest freely eat; but of the tree of the knowledge of good and evil, thou shalt not eat of it; for in the day that thou eatest thereof, thou shalt surely die,"[110]—these words are clear and require no exegesis. But the devil insisted on "exegesis": "Yea, hath God said?"[111] So it was in the days of the Reformation. Luther took his stand on the clear words of the Sacrament. "The words," he said, "are too powerful as they stand." Zwingli and his associates suggested that our Church either *remove entirely out of sight* the words of institution as being obscure, and draw the doctrine of the Lord's Supper from other texts, or, if the obscure words

---

[109] St. L. Ed. XII, 1174.

[110] Gen. 2, 16. 17.

[111] Gen, 3, 1.

are to be kept in view, *"interpret"* them in such a way as to bring them into harmony with the *Reformed* notion of Christ's ascension and His sitting at the right hand of God. As noted before, Luther, during the Marburg Colloquy, so as not to have his true perspective disturbed, wrote with crayon on the table before him: *Hoc est corups meum.* The same question of principle is involved in all controversies of our day, and will be to the end of time. When the devil desires to bring about division and offense in the Church, he does not come like the devil he is, but goes to the Scriptures. He either quotes texts that are irrelevant,[112] or ventures to offer exegesis.[113] If the Lutheran Church in America would, therefore, reap the benefit of the recent controversy, it should learn, and resolve never to forget, this truth: The Christian Church can and ought to stand solely on *the World of Christ*, and on no gloss. The Lord Jesus does not say: If ye remain in the *interpretation* of my Word, but: "If ye continue in my *Word*, then are ye my disciples indeed; and ye shall know the truth, and the truth shall make you free."[114] By abandoning the Scriptures and substituting for them human constructions, we must suffer the loss of the Christian principle of knowledge and the glorious liberty of the children of God. By abandoning the Word of Scripture, we *err* and become *servants of men*. To quote Luther: "When the devil has once succeeded in removing the *Word* from heart and eye, and induced us to make our own thoughts about articles of faith, without the Word, we are lost."[115] Let us not be mistaken as to the real state of things! Even among church people sayings like this have obtained some currency: "All church-bodies stand on the Scriptures, and differ only in their *interpretation*." That is not true! The Roman Church does not stand on the Scriptures, but on the Roman *interpretation* of the Scriptures. The Reformed bodies do not stand on the Scriptures, so far as they differ from us, but on Zwingli's, Calvin's, etc., *interpretation* of the Scriptures. The Lutheran Church, on the other hand, does not stand on interpretations of Scripture, but

---

[112] Matt. 4, 5—7.

[113] Gen. 3, 1.

[114] John 8, 31. 32.

[115] St. L. Ed. V, 455.

on Scripture itself. How gloriously would the American Lutheran Church fulfill its mission here in America, standing like an unshaken rock in the midst of the billows of sectarianism, if it took its stand, as one man, on the clear Word, and bore witness to the clear Word! There Luther's strength lay. There must remain the strength of Lutheranism, over against all sectarian formations, until Judgement Day. Luther wrote from the Wartburg: "It is enough that *we* have Scripture; *they* have not Scripture."[116] And again: "Behold, ye may refute all writings of papists with ease, though each of them wrote a hundred thousand books; for, as I have said, they are, to a man, *Scripture-less*, rude, unlearned writers, who had more properly become servants in a bathhouse than controversialists. *Let no one lead you away from and out of Scripture*, however hard they may try. For if ye abandon it, ye are lost; they will lead you whither they will. But if ye remain in it (in Scripture), ye have won and need be concerned about their raging as little as the rock is concerned about the waves and billows of the sea. What they write is mere waves and surges. Be quite assured and do not doubt, there is nothing more luminous than the sun, that is to say, the Scriptures."[117]

---

[116] St. L. Ed. V, 310.

[117] St. L. Ed. V, 337.

10

Preparation for Conversion

X. Preparation (Praeparatio) for Conversion.

It is permissible to speak of a "preparation" for conversion and of "acts preparatory" (*actus praeparatorii*) to conversion? It is necessary that we reach a mutual understanding in regard to this point. Since the seventies of the last century it has come up for discussion, and has quite recently been brought forward again in *Kirketidende*.

Two things must be stated regarding this matter: 1. It accords with the facts in the case, and is quite Scriptural, to speak of a "preparation" for conversion. 2. It is a fact that Semi-Pelagians and synergists have ever used the term "preparation" as a repository for their notions of man's merit and man's cooperation for conversion. Accordingly, theologians who are careful about their language, from Chemnitz to our own day, adopt this course, *viz.,* they retain the expression "preparation" as in accord with Scripture and the facts in the case, but reject the error which hides under the correct expression.

We are face to face with *error* in every instance where we meet with the teaching that *man* in some way prepares, or is able to prepare, himself for conversion. The words: "So, then, it is not of him that willeth, nor of him that runneth, but of God that showeth mercy,"[118] apply to *anything* that man can do or omit doing before his conversion, also to his outward integrity and the external hearing and study of the Bible. Very properly, therefore, the Formula of Concord rejects the teaching that man, when grace is offered to him, in any way "can qualify and prepare himself for grace."[119] On the other hand, it is correct and Scriptural to say that *God* prepares man for conversion. Conversion in the strict and narrower sense consists in the bestowal of faith in Christ. "And a great number believed and turned unto God."[120] With still greater clearness the fact that being converted is brought about by becoming a believer is stated by the Greek text: πολύς τε ἀριθμὸς ὁ πιστεύσας. Faith in the Gospel, however, originates only *after* God has be the Law, worked a knowledge of sin. Even in instances of sudden conversion, so-called, as, for instance, in the sudden conversion of the Apostle Paul (which, by the way, took place not *in* Damascus, but *on the road* to Damascus), the knowledge of sin worked by the Law preceded faith in point of time. Luther was accustomed to express this matter thus: Man will not flee to Christ unless he has *first* tasted hell. And this having-tasted-hell is a necessary *praeparatio* for conversion. In this sense the Scriptures call the Law a "schoolmaster to bring us unto Christ": ὁ νομος παιδαγωγός ἡμῶν γέγονεν εἰς Χριστόν.[121] The Law is not *in itself* a schoolmaster unto Christ, or a guide unto Christ. In itself the Law only works either self-righteousness or despair, thus making man a fugitive from Christ. But when employed by *God*, the Law becomes a schoolmaster unto Christ, and prepares the way for Christ and the Gospel. Luther comments on Gal. 3, 24. 25: "The Law prepares for grace (*ad gratiam praeparat*) by revealing and augmenting sin and by humiliating the proud, in order that they may desire help from Christ."[122] *Chemnitz* stigmatizes as

---

[118] Rom. 9, 16.

[119] Mueller, p. 525, § 11. Jacobs, p. 498.

[120] Acts 11, 21.

[121] Gal. 3, 24.

[122] Lex, ut dixi, ad gratiam praeparat, dum peccatum revelat et auget, humilians superbos ad auxilium Christi desiderandum. (Opp. Erl. III, 300. St. L. Ed. VIII, 1504).

slander the Romanist charge that the Lutherans taught no "preparation" for the acceptance of justifying grace. He says: "It is untrue when they charge in the 9th canon[123] that we deny that any motions of the will, imparted and quickened by God, precede the acceptance of justification. For we do teach that repentance or contrition come first, and these cannot exist without great, sincere, and earnest motions of the will. But we do not say that penitence or contrition precede as something meritorious."[124] This statement of Chemnitz is preceded by another, as follows: "If they (the Romanists) would ascribe what according to the Scriptures precedes, not to human energies, but to the grace of God and the working of the Spirit, and would not, because of these preparations, set up a claim of a merit or worthiness on account of which we are justified, we could easily come to an agreement about the word 'preparation,' correctly understood according to the Scripture. Nor did Luther show an aversion to this word. He says, commenting on the 3rd chapter of Galatians: The Law in its proper office serves grace and prepares for grace (*esse praeparatricem ad gratiam*), because it serves to open up an entrance (*aditum*) to us for grace. Indeed, he goes so far as to say that the Law in its office may subserve justification, not because it justifies, but because it drives (*urgeat*) man toward the promises of grace and makes these sweet and desirable."

It is a patent fact, however, that the Scriptural term "preparation" has been *misused*. The Romanists as well as the synergists, of early and recent times, have used the expression in order to teach *man's cooperation* in his own conversion, justification, and salvation. The *Roman* doctrine, as is well known, is this: If man does what he can by means of his natural powers, God gives him grace. They called this human activity, which guarantees to man the grace of God, *meritum congrui*, merit by fairness. It were but fair, the Scholastics said, that God would grant His grace to those who did as

---

[123] The 9th Canon (Sess. 6. Conc. Trid.) reads as follows: Si quis dixerit, sola fide impium justificari, ita ut intelligat nihil aliud requiri, quod ad justificationis gratiam consequendam cooperatur, et nulla ex parte necesse esse, eum suae coluntatis motu praeparari atque disponi: anathema sit. (Ed. Smets, p. 33).

[124] Examen Conc. Trid., p. m. 156.

much as lay in their powers. After the Reformation the Romanists began to be ashamed of the word "merit." For *meritum congrui* they substituted the word "preparation"—*praeparatio* or *dispositio*. Man mus be "prepared" or "disposed" for the acceptance of divine grace. It is Chemnitz, again, in his *Examen* of the canons of the Council of Trent, who proves in a very thorough manner that the Romanists understand by *praeparatio* exactly the same thing which they had formerly designated as "merit by fairness" "Mark well," he addresses the reader, "that by the expression 'preparation' or 'disposition' (*vocabulo praeparationis et dispositionis*) the Council of Trent understands the same as that which the Scholastic theologians used to teach by means of the term 'merit by fairness,' *meritum congrui*."[125]

But also within the Lutheran Church the word "preparation" has been employed in an effort to cover up human merit and man's cooperation in conversion. In the seventeenth century, Latermann, Musaeus, and their respective associates ascribed to man, *before* conversion, a self-decision for grace, a good conduct over against grace, a desire for grace, a cooperation unto conversion. Charged with Semi-Pelagianism and synergism by the dogmaticians, they, too, sought refuge in *praeparatio*. They asserted that when referring to a self-decision in favor of conversion, a willing of conversion, cooperation unto conversion, etc., they did not mean a natural will, but a will *prepared* (*coluntatem praeparatam*) by grace. The dogmaticians point out the deception here involved. "Latermann indeed claims," says Quenstedt, "that man cooperates with divine grace in conversion by means of powers which God gives him, and that he presupposes a will *prepared* by God. But he says nothing that the Jesuits, Bellarminus, and others, have not said, who have nevertheless been accused of Pelagianism and Semi-Pelagianism by all our theologians; he says nothing that has not been claimed by the synergists. They, too, presuppose the gift of grace, and loudly insist that they assume a will *prepared* by God."[126] We are forced to remind our readers of things, and, in part, to repeat quotations, which we have pointed out in a previous

---

[125] Examen, p.m. 156.

[126] Systema, II, 726.

chapter. The dogmaticians advanced a twofold argument against Latermann. First: A will "prepared" in such a way that it can *decide* in favor of grace, and can *will* grace, is already converted. Secondly: When Latermann speaks of a self-decision for conversion, he does not mean a decision by means of powers conveyed by grace, but by natural powers. The Strassburg Faculty, quoted before, askes Latermann to consider the following facts: What manner of human power is that which it rests…whether a person wills his conversion and also wills not to be converted, as Latermann says? He will not say that these are the powers and ability conferred by the Holy Ghost. For what sort of declaration would this be: It rests with the *new* powers and *imparted* faculties to furnish, or not to furnish, that which is necessary for conversion, to will, or not to will, conversion! Are these new powers, then *indifferent* as regards conversion or rejection, willing and not-willing? There must be a *previous to* the imparting of powers by the Spirit a faculty *in man* by means of which, with the aid of superadded grace, that which is necessary for conversion is performed, by means of which man is brought to will conversion. And that is Pelagianism and synergism."[127] Just so Dr. Stellhorn, in 1872, as mentioned above argued against the Iowaans that they violated the doctrine of original depravity by teaching: Hence the cause why one is lost and the other saved bust be sought in the dissimilar conduct of man over against proffered grace, in the individual personal decision.

In view of such misuse of the term "preparation" and "preparatory acts," the question suggests itself whether it were not best to reject these expressions entirely and to outlaw them from theology. But this will not do, as it would involve a departure from the Scriptures. We have noted above that the operations of the Law which precede the working of faith are subsumed in Scripture under the notion of "preparation." Chemnitz here indicates the right mode of procedure. He does not reject the term "preparation" on account of its abuse at the hands of the Romanists, but proceeds to rule out the false conceptions which the Romanists have introduced into the term. Just so the later dogmaticians over against Latermann and Musaeus.

---

[127] Quoted by Calov, X, 50.

Dr. Walther employed the same terminology, as when he says: "Conversion, indeed, does not occur ordinarily without several preparatory phenomena (*Vorgaenge*) within man, and in this sense conversion is accomplished by degrees, gradually; but conversion itself in every case occurs *in an instant*."[128] The dogmaticians take issue with Latermann and Musaeus on account of their doctrine of " a will *prepared* by grace" in the sense that man *decides* for conversion, is able to *will or not to will* conversion. But they themselves speak of "preparatory acts" (*actus praeparatorii*), in the sense, however, that not *man* prepares himself for conversion, but that *God* leads man to conversion. Under all *actus praeparatorii* man remains spiritually dead, *subjectum convertendum*; he never becomes *active* under the preparatory acts, but merely experiences influences *from without.* The dogmaticians present the matter as follows: Conversion, in the real and narrow sense of the word, so far as it consists in the kindling of faith, is *never* a process, but always occurs *in a moment* (*conversio semper momentanea est*). There is no such thing as a *status medius* between death and life, between the converted and the unconverted state. In what sense, then, can our theologians still speak of "preparatory acts"? They concede that, as in the instance of Paul, God could work every conversion in a moment, without "preparatory acts" extending over days, weeks, months, possibly years. But as a rule, God *is pleased* to proceed differently. "It pleases the Holy Spirit," says Quenstedt, "according to His free will, to proceed not always by means of a sudden commotion as in the conversion of Paul, but more frequently by slow and successive degrees."[129] It must be admitted that this statement is materially correct. As regards the element of time God needs no preparatory stage. He is able to convert every sinner instantaneously, even in the very commission, externally, of some infamy, and in external outbursts of malice. Thus Paul was converted in the midst of persecuting fury, when he was "exceedingly mad," when his hands were gory with the blood of Christians and eager to shed it anew. Thus, according to ancient report, a pagan actor

---

[128] Noerdlicher Bericht, 1873, p.36.

[129] Systema, II, 707: Placet Spiritui S. pro libera sua voluntate non semper motu subitaneo, ut in conversione Pauli factum, sed frequentius lente et successive hic progredi.

was suddenly converted while he was acting a travesty on the sacrament of Baptism. Thus Dr. Sihler, as related by him in private company and recorded by him somewhere, experienced a sudden conversion.[130] Persons thus converted are able to state the exact time of their conversion. But in most cases the outward course observable in conversion is a different one. Most converted persons have not been converted at the first contact with the Word of God. They receive impressions of the operations of the Law and Gospel extending through a longer or shorter period of time. They experience motion (*motus*) which through their own fault remain ineffectual. But the Lord does not yet turn away from them. He continues to work upon their hearts by His Holy Spirit through the Word. When, finally, the moment arrives which God has determined[131] for the enkindling of faith, the change of a will utterly opposed to the Gospel into a will assenting to the Gospel is wrought in a way imperceptible to human feeling, and so divinely gentle that few converted persons are able to state the hour of its occurrence; as Chemnitz says: they are unable to state the moment when the natural acts (*actus animales*) were turned into spiritual acts (*actus spirituales*), or when the *liberated* will (*voluntas liberata*) became active.[132]

What manner of *motus* in man, then, *precede* conversion? Later dog-

---

[130] Our attention has been called to the fact that an account of Dr. Sihler's sudden conversion is found in his autobiography, Vol. I, p.82, as follows: "During a lecture I had again been seized by an overmastering passion. After I had returned to my room, God struck me a terrible blow, hurling me kneeling and prostrate to the ground. I was being bruised with the hammer of His Law so utterly that I could not hear nor see anything else (than His wrath). In a twinkling I felt and knew in my inmost heart and conscience that I had shamefully transgressed not only the fifth, but every other commandment, and that from the crown of my head to the sole of my foot, from my skin to the marrow in my bones, I was a miserable, lost cursed, and condemned sinner who had merited eternal pain and torment in the abyss of hell. Still our gracious and merciful God did not suffer me to sink and perish utterly in these terrors of hell, but plucked me out of them with His might, and revealed to me that the true Christ, the Christ of the Bible, His own and Mary's Son, was my Savior too, and thus kindled in me true faith in Him. And this, too, was done in a trice, with lightning rapidity."

[131] F. C., Sol. Decl. Mueller, p. 716, § 56. Jacobs, p. 659.

[132] L. de lib. arb., p.m. 490.

maticians here, over against Latermann and Musaeus, use a more exact terminology than the earlier theologians. Chemnitz had occasionally spoken of *"pious"* motions *before* conversion, as when he says: "After the Holy Spirit has called forth a *holy* intention, wish, or endeavor, it does not rest with *us* to change our will in the direction of something better, but God works in us to will."[133] Calovius and Quenstedt, on the other hand, in opposition to the teaching of Musaeus, reject the doctrine that, *before* conversion is consummate, "*good* motions, *holy* thoughts, *pious* longings, *good* endeavors," awakened by prevenient grace, may be attributed to man. The Holy Spirit indeed calls forth motions before conversion. And if their origin (*causa efficiens*) be urged, one might call them spiritual motions. But since man's hostile will, before conversion is accomplished, has yet undergone no *change*, it will not do, *with reference to man*, to speak of "pious" or "holy" motions at this stage. We have quoted before the words of Quenstedt and Calovius: "Where there are such motions" (*viz.*, good motions, holy thoughts, pious desires), "man is already roused from death, already lives by virtue of spiritual life, and hence is already converted."[134] Of the later dogmaticians, Calovius before others gives luminous and clear-cut expression to the truth that before a person's conversion is accomplished for the first time, no *spiritual* motions can be ascribed to him. He says: "Though unconverted persons at times gladly hear the messengers of the Word, this is because of the outward talents of the latter, or from some other *carnal* desire (*ob aliam quamvis cupiditatem carnalem*), as in the case of Herod, Mark 6, 7, and is not due to an inclination for the Word of God (*ob affectum erga Dei verbum*), since such inclination is a product of faith (*e fide redundat*), whcih originates only from hearing the Word, Rom. 10, 17. Before conversion there is no such spiritual desire (*desiderium spirituale*) nor any such inclination towards the divine Word, because the Word is *foolishness* to natural man, and meets with his resistance,

---

[133] Loci; locus de libero arb., p.m. 484: Postquam excitavit Spiritus S. pium propositum, desiderium, conatum, non est in nostra potestate mutare voluntatem in melius, sed Deus operatur in nobis velle.

[134] Quenstedt, Systema, II, 729.

1 Cor. 2, 14; Rom. 8, 7."[135] And again: "If in the unconverted man pious motions, holy thoughts, beginnings of faith, a struggle of the spirit against the flesh are *imagined* (*finguntur*), this involves a self-contradiction; for where such motions occur, man is awakened from death and already lives through spiritual life... Briefly: 1. To assume holy thoughts previous to regeneration, conversion, and faith, is pure and genuine Pelagianism. 2. To assume holy motions previous to the work of the Holy Spirit, places the effect before the cause. 3. To assume in the corrupt heart of non-converted man a pious longing, amounts to producing good fruit while the tree is still corrupt. 4. To imagine, in him, a struggle of the flesh with the Spirit, is a contradiction in terms. 5. To assume the beginnings of faith where regeneration has not occurred, when, in fact, faith originates through regeneration, is the same as assuming the child to exist before the father."[136] And still there is no material contradiction between Calovius and Chemnitz. Although Chemnitz refers to a "pious" desire (*pium desiderium*) called forth by the Holy Spirit before conversion, he is careful at once to add: "It is not within our power to change our will in the direction of something better" (*non est in nostra porestate mutare voluntatem in melius*). Chemnitz, accordingly has in mind only such motions as are produced by the Holy Spirit *from without*, by means of which, however, man *receives as his own* no spiritual powers by means of which he were able to *conduct himself rightly* and desire conversion. Hence Luthardt's remark that Calovius in his rejection of all cooperation in conversion goes even beyond the Formula of Concord (*sc.* Chemnitz), is not well taken.[137] That Chemnitz's *pium desiderium* before conversion has reference only to motions which are produced by the Holy Spirit *from without*, and by no means refers to motions which man has received as his *own* through an *indwelling* spiritual power, is clear from the fact that he expressly terms these motions "natural" ones (*naturales*), as distinguished from the "spiritual" (*spirituales*), when he says that man has no cognizance of the moment when the *operationes animales* change

---

[135] Systema, X, 23.

[136] Systema, X, 146. 149.

[137] Die Lehre vom dreien Willen, p. 302.

PREPARATION FOR CONVERSION

into *operationes spirituales*.

With reference to the motions produced in man previous to conversion, Dr. Walther would use various *illustrations*, the illustration, *e. g.*, of a besieged fortress. The fortress receives impressions from without: it is bombarded and attacked. The besieged, however, do not make common cause with the besieging force, but try to prevent the taking of the fortress. Then, the image of an India-runner ball which receives pressure from without. When the pressure from without ceases, the ball resumes its former shape.[138] "Not until man has yielded to the operations of God, when grace is no longer merely working from without (*gratia assistens*), but indwelling in him, man may cooperate. Whoever teaches otherwise can do so only from *Pelagian premises*."[139] With reference to the motions produced in the non-converted, the *motus inevitabiles*, as he is willing to call them, Walther cites Acts 26, 28 (King Agrippa); Luke 4, 22 (the inhabitants of Nazareth); Acts 24, 25 (Felix); and others. Quite properly so. It will not do to interpret Acts 26, 28, "Almost thou persuadest me to be a Christian," as *irony*. The entire context forbids such interpretation. Paul had addressed Agrippa with mighty words concerning his conversion, and the death and resurrection of Christ according to the prophets. Paul then turns directly to Agrippa and asks him, "King Agrippa, believest thou the prophets? I know that thou believest!" Then Agrippa replied, "Almost thou persuadest me to become a Christian." The context shows that the whole company was listening attentively, and that Festus and Agrippa were were really inwardly moved and powerfully agitated. Such was Paul's impression, too, for upon Agrippa's exclamation, "Almost thou persuadest me to be a Christian," he replied, "I would to God that not only thou, but also all thay hear me this day were both almost and altogether such as I am, except these bonds." The concluding words, too, vv. 30-32, where the high dignitaries, "talking among themselves," argued that Paul might be released, do not indicate irony. The case of Felix, Acts 24, 25, is just as clear. When Paul was speaking of justice and chastity and the

---

[138] Noerdlicher Distrikt, 1873, pp. 51 sq.

[139] Noerdlicher Distrikt, 1873, pp. 51 sq.

future judgement, Felix was frightened, he "trembled" (ἔμφοβος γενόμενος). Palpably the *motus inevitablies*. But likewise *motus non irresistibiles*, for Felix suppressed the motions and said, "Go thy way for this time; when I have a convenient time, I will call for thee." He hoped also that money should be given him of Paul. Walther remarks: "That man cannot prevent his being affected by the Word of God is shown by the example of Felix, who was not at all inclined to be affected, for he heard Paul in the hope of getting money from him. He could not evade the effect of the sermon of the Law; he trembled. But he was able to resist, and dismissed the apostle with the words, 'Go thy way for this time.'"[140] Also in the preaching of the Law the Holy Spirit is active and convicts man of the wrath of God against sin. And this is accompanied by "great, genuine, and earnest motions (*motus*) of the will," says Chemnitz.[141] Again, that the *Gospel* causes motions in the heart of man even before conversion is clear from Luke 4, 22. The Lord preached a powerful Gospel sermon in the synagogue at Nazareth. He read Is. 61, 1, dealing with the purpose and aim of the Messiah's appearing: Messiah is sent "to preach the Gospel to the poor, to heal the broken-hearted, to preach deliverance to the captives and recovering of sight to the blind, to set at liberty them that are bruised, to preach the acceptable year of the Lord." He returns the scroll to the servant and commences to speak while all eyes are directed upon Him (ἀτενίζοντες). He applies the passage Is. 61, not like De Wette, to the mission of Isaiah "to the captives in exile," but to Himself, to Jesus of Nazareth: "This day is this scripture fulfilled in your ears." He held forth with much power the Gospel, the acceptable year of the Lord, which had been inaugurated by His coming. And the people of Nazareth were impressed. The impression is described as follows: "And all bare Him witness, and wondered at the gracious words (ἐπὶ τοῖς λόγοις τῆς χάριτος) which proceeded out of His mouth." However, in spite of being thus impressed, these people were not yet converted, as is clear from the fact that they rose up like one man when Christ touched their Jewish pride, and wanted to cast Him from the

---

[140] L. c., p. 48.

[141] Examen, De fide justif., p. 156.

brow of the hill.[142] Nor will it do to interpret Mark 12, 34, "Thou art not far from the kingdom of God," as signifying, "Thou art already *in* the kingdom of God." Some have urged this meaning in an effort to show that a "moral, just disposition" qualifies for the kingdom of God.[143] Others had an opposite interest in urging this interpretation, *viz.*, to exclude from the start every thought of *praeparatio* for the entrance into the kingdom of God. In order to justify the interpretation, "Thou art already *in* the kingdom of God," Acts 17, 27 has been appealed to, where Paul says that the Lord "is not far from every one of us." In this passage, in Acts 17, a litotes must indeed be recognized. By saying, "God is not far from us," the apostle intends to say, "God is very near to us, we are *in* God." But the apostle *himself* says that his words in this place should be understood by litotes, for he adds: "For *in* Him we life, and move, and have our being." As a corresponding explanation is lacking in the text of Mark 12, it is not advisable to add one, but the words should be taken as they read, without a figure of speech, thus: "Thou art not far from the kingdom of God." The act of being led to the kingdom of God is here conceived as a stretch of road or a process where one is nearer the goal than the other. Here, too, the context shows how "not far," (οὐ μαχράν), is to be understood. The scribe no longer criticized Jesus, but was even now impressed by the words of the Lord, observing that He had answered the Sadducees "well" (χαλῶς). Then, too, he had gained the knowledge that the real content of the Law is to love God with all our hear and our neighbor as ourselves. He had given up the delusion that by the outward accomplishment of the works demanded by God, burnt offerings and sacrifices, v. 33, the Law of God is kept. In this condition the scribe was not yet *in* the kingdom of God, still he was nearer the kingdom than those scribes who believed that their outward performance of the works demanded by the Lord was a fulfillment of the Law, and who merely criticized the Lord's sayings. Dr. Walther remarks: "When the Lord says: 'Thou art not far from the kingdom of God,' Mark 12, 34, He would say: There are in thee even now preparatory effects of the Spirit; for the

---

[142] Cp. Bericht des Noerdlichen Distrikts, 1873, p. 49.

[143] As, e. g., De Wette in l. See the refutation in Olshausen on Matt. 22, 40.

scribe here addressed had already yielded to a better understanding of the Law." But in the same connection Walther rejects every *status medius*. He says: "Whoever teaches that a man may be converted, and yet not be entirely converted, contradicts the Scriptures, which know but two states, death or life. Whoever is no under grace is under wrath; whoever is not in life is still in death; whoever is not on the way to heaven is on the way to hell; whoever is an unsaved person is a damned person. There is no twilight stage, no middle state between light and darkness."[144]

In order, then, not to be compelled to use forced interpretations of Scripture, it should be maintained, on the one hand, that there is indeed a "preparation" for conversion. On the other hand, it is to be maintained with equal emphasis that only by the enkindling of faith spiritual life enters into man, and that under all "preparatory acts" man remains spiritually dead, *subjectum convertendum*. There are indeed previous to conversion *motus "from* the Holy Spirit, but not *with* the Holy Spirit." These *motus* may be termed "spiritual" or "good" motions only inasmuch as they are called forth by the Holy Spirit, but *viewed from the standpoint of the condition of man, whose will is still at enmity with God,* they are *carnales* or *animales*, as expressed by Chemnitz and Calovius. "It sounds very fine," says Walther, "when modern theologians say: When God gives strength to unconverted man, he is able to cooperate towards his conversion. But that is wrong; for a dead person cannot make use of imparted powers as long as he lacks the strength necessary for the employment of such powers, that is to say, as long as he lacks life. You may roll a dead body back and forth, and by applying electricity cause him to open his eyes or his mouth, and so on, but all this remains a result of forces affecting him *from without*. Only he who has become subjectively a possessor

---

[144] L. c., p. 42.

of power can move himself."[145]

Adverting once more to the Norwegian Articles of Agreement, we would in this connection, urge that the wording of Thesis 5d should not be censured, but should be acknowledged as correct. Thesis 5d *rejects* the teaching that faith "is the result of a power or ability imparted to man by the call of grace and therefore now dwelling in, and belonging to, unregenerate man, to decide himself for grace." According to the wording of this thesis, two facts are here expressed: There are motions in man called forth by the Holy Spirit before conversion; divine powers are operating on man before conversion, but man is not able, by virtue of such powers, to decide for the Gospel, because these powers are not yet indwelling in him, have not yet become his own.

---

[145] *Noerdlicher Bericht*, 1873, p.53. Also the term *refrenatio,* as used by Walther and our old theologians, does not denote an *inner* transformation (which, indeed, is not the meaning of the word), but is used with reference to the *outward* "restraining" of the grosser outbursts of the flesh. This outward check on the flesh is an effect of the Law prior to a person's believing, and has the purpose of keeping man outwardly to be a hearer of the Word. The expression and its cannotated subject-matter is not peculiar to the dogmaticians, but is found also in Luther, Chemnitz, and the Confessions (the abstaining from outward sins, *peccatis absinere,* effected by the Law *previous* to the enkindling of faith). In our writings, *refrenatio* is frequently translated "taming," *Zaehmung*; somewhat inexactly, as "taming" *may* indicate a sort of inner change. *Refrenatio* should be translated "restraining" or "checking," *Zeugelung*. *Furit concupiscentia,* says Luther, *et odit legem, carcerem suum, sed cogitur tamen ab OPERIBUS absinere peccati.* Cp. Chemnitx, *Examen*; De fide justif., p. 155. F. C., Mueller, p. 634, § 8. Jacobs, p. 590.

11

The Possibility of Conversion

IX. The "Possibility of Conversion.

Is it proper to speak of a "possibility of conversion," "an opportunity of conversion," "the possibility of becoming converted," or "the possibility of converting oneself"? Also these terms have again become subjects of discussion, pursuant to the Norwegian Articles of Agreement, and an understanding must be reached with reference to them if a unity on a Scriptural and confessional basis is to be attained. Here, too, a twofold statement is to be made: 1. It is in agreement with the facts, and Biblically correct, to speak of a "*possibility* of conversion," etc. 2. It is a fact that this correct expression has been employed in former and recent times in an effort to palm off the notion of human cooperation in conversion. We take the proper stand by retaining the expression, but, at the same time, pointing out and rejecting the error which would hide under this Scriptural expression.

In Is. 55, 6: "Seek ye the Lord while He may be found," the thought is conveyed: Seek the Lord while He *can* be found, while it is *possible* to believe in Him, while there is a *possibility* of faith in Him. Hence we find not only among the dogmaticians of the seventeenth century, but also among the sixteenth century theologians, the statement that with the Gospel is given a "possibility" and "opportunity" of conversion, simply because the expression has Scriptural warrant. Lucas Osiander, commenting on Is. 55, 6, says: Tum Dominus prope est et inveniri *potest*, cum per evangelii praedicationem nobis salutem offert. Cum autem verbum suum aufert, ut non amplius rectae agnoscatur, tunc nec inveniri neque recte incocari potest. Quare gratia mente *occasionem*, qua Dominus ad nos clementer accedit, arripiamus. That is to say: "The Lord is near and *can* be found when through the preaching of the Gospel He offers salvation to us. But when He takes away His Word, so that it no longer is correctly understood, He can be neither found nor properly worshiped. Let us, then, gratefully seize the *opportunity* by means of which the Lord in His grace approaches us." This manner of speaking has found its way into our Confession, where we read: "Such calling through the preaching of the Word we ought not to regard as a delusion, but know that God thereby reveals His will, that He would, by means of the Word, work upon those whom He thus calls, that they *might be* enlightened, converted, and saved."[146] The expressions, "possibility of conversion," "opportunity" of conversion, "possibility of being converted," should, then, be retained *in this sense, viz.,* that the saving grace of God comprises all men, that the Holy Spirit operates in all hearers unto conversion, and that the cause of non-conversion is to be sought solely in man's resistance. This is summed up in the term *gratia sufficiens*. The Scriptures teach *gratia sufficiens*, that is to say, it teaches that God operates through the call in such a manner and *to such an extent* that *all* hearers of the Word "may be enlightened, converted, and saved," and that no hearer remains unconverted by reason of some deficiency in the operations of divine grace or by reason of a lack of gracious intent on the part of God. Is. 5, 4 the Lord says with reference to the disobedient people: "What could have been done more to my vineyard that I have not done to it?" Matt. 23, 37 Christ testifies against Jerusalem: "How often would I have gathered thy children together!" And this He had desired not only perfunctorily, but as earnestly and eagerly "as a hen gathereth her chickens under her wings; and ye would not!" Acts 7, 51 Stephen, in his address before the council, sums up the situation thus: "Ye do always resist the Holy Ghost," (τῷ πνεύματι τῷ

---

[146] Mueller, p. 710 § 29. Jacobs, p. 654.

ἁγίῳ ἀντιπίπτετε), ye fall foul of the Holy Spirit. According to these texts, determined resistance is required to prevent the blessed result of the Holy Spirit's operations. No *misuse* of the expression, "possibility of conversion," aptly termed the "objective" possibility, should induce us to abandon this expression or to pronounce it incorrect. The objetive possibility for all who live under the sound of the Word to become converted demarcates Lutheran from Calvinistic doctrine. It is but another term for *gratia universalis, seria et efficax*. Because Calvin rejects the universality of grace, he stoutly denies the existence of a possibility of conversion for all hearers of the Word, and insists with great emphasis that by His calling the Lord offers to part of the hearers merely the possibility and opportunity *of bringing upon themselves a greater damnation*.[147]

On the other hand, we must guard against the *synergism* which may lurk in the formula "possibility of conversion." Synergism views "possibility as a *limitation*. Its teaching is to this effect, that God merely makes *possible* conversion. Whether conversion will proceed beyond the degree of possibility and become an *actuality*, whether man will *actually* be converted, depends upon the fact that *man* before his conversion does something,— and, indeed, the *decisive* part,— viz., upon man's right conduct over against grace, the cessation of willful resistance, his decision for conversion, etc. This is the view of modern German theologians, as, for instance, of Luthardt.[148] This is the view also of the American Lutherans who have stood opposed to the Synodical Conference. Dr. Schmidt, in a discussion of Is. 5, 4, remarks: "God says, 'What could have been done more to my vineyard that I have not done in

---

[147] *Institutiones*, III, 24, 8: Est enim universalis vocation, qua per externam verbi praedicationem omnes pariter ad se invitat Deus, *etiam quibus eam in mortis odorem et gravioris condemnationis materiam proponit*. And again, III, 24, 12: Quos ergo in vitae contumeliam et mortis exitium *creavit*, ut irae suae organa forent et severitatis exempla, eos, ut in finem suum perveniant, nunc audiendi verbi sui facultate privat, *nunc ejus praedicatione magis excaecat et obstupefacit*.

[148] *Die Lehre vom freien Willen*, p. 276. Just so in his last dogmatical work, *Die christliche Glaubenslehre*, 1898, p. 442: "The determining influence (of God) does not take the place of self-decision; rather, it moves only to the boundaries of self-decision. Self-decision is not taken away from, or rendered unnecessary for, man; it is, however, made possible for him."

it?' Now, then, if *nothing* more remains for God to do, who but unconverted man himself must on his part do something to be converted and saved?"[149] This is the synergistic conception: God offers to man the powers of grace for his conversion. Without such offer conversion were inconceivable. But by virtue of his condition before conversion unconverted man is *able* to do so much,—may and must do so much,— that he *rightly uses* the energies imparted by grace, decides in favor of conversion, conducts himself rightly over against grace, ceases to resist willfully, and so on. In a word, synergism turns the objective possibility of conversion into a *subjective* ability of man *before* conversion. The synergist with *his* "possibility of conversion" maintains an antithesis to all texts of Scripture which represent man as *dead* in sins (νεκροὺς τοῖς παραπτώμασιν), and *hostile* to the Gospel (μωρία γὰρ αὐτῷ ἐστίν), and which deny any *subjective possibility* of faith on his part (οὐ δύναται γνῶναι).[150] Moreover, the synergist's "possibility of conversion" contradicts all passages of Scripture which ascribe conversion or faith itself—not only the power to believe—solely to the operations of divine grace and omnipotence, without any cooperation on the part of man. Eph. 1, 19.20: "We *believe*" (πιστεύοντες)—not merely: we are *able to* believe—"according to the working of His mighty power." Phil. 1, 29: "Unto you it is given on behalf of Christ…to believe on Him" (τὸ εἰς αὐτὸν πιστεύειν), not merely, the *ability* to believe on Him. In thus placing man's subjective ability before conversion, the synergist maintains a position contradictory not only of the position of the sixteenth century theologians of our Church, but also of that of the seventeenth century dogmaticians. As we have noted above, the latter, too, emphatically maintain, over against Latermann and Musaeus, that God works, without human cooperation, not only the possibility of conversion, but also conversion itself, works not only the *ability* to will, but causes man *to will*. The Strassburg Faculty: "Does not God, on His part, grant that we *will*? that we *believe*? Does He merely grant that we are *able* to will, *able* to convert ourselves, *able*

---

[149] *A.u.N.V,* 224.

[150] Eph. 2, 1; 1 Cor. 2, 14.

to believe?"[151] We must hold fast, on the basis of Scripture: when man is inwardly or *subjectively* changed to such a degree as to be *able* to accept grace, he is no longer the old, natural man who regards the Gospel as foolishness, but is a new man, completely transformed within, who has, through the operations of the Holy Spirit, learned to regard the Gospel as the wisdom of God. Viewing man's *subjective* condition, our Confession says concerning conversion, not concerning a stage *introductory* to conversion: *"Conversion is a change of man's mind, heart, and will wrought by the Holy Spirit, so that man is able through such operation of the Holy Spirit to accept proffered grace (potest oblatam gratiam apprehendere)."*[152]

In order, then, to be united on a Scriptural basis, it is necessary to maintain over against Calvinism the *objective* possibility of conversion for every hearer of the Word, and to reject over against synergism all subjective *I can* on the part of man before conversion. Only by doing this do we hold fast *universalis gratia* on the one hand and *sola gratia* on the other.

---

[151] Quoted by Calov, X, 50.

[152] Mueller, p. 608, § 83. Jacobs, p. 568.

12

Two Concepts of Calling

XII. The Two Concepts of Calling.

Without questioning, "calling" is used in a twofold sense in Scripture. Rom. 1, 6 "the called of Jesus Christ," κλητοὶ Ἰησοῦ Χριστοῦ, are the *converted* of Jesus Christ, those actually received into the kingdom of God, the *Christians*. Being called is here identical with being converted or becoming a believer. And this is certainly the meaning of the term in the great majority of passages in the epistles. On the other hand, Matt. 22, 14: "Many are called, but few are chosen," (πολλοί γάρ εἰσιν χλητοί, ὀλίγοι δέ ἐλεχτοί, *distinguishes* the call from the elect. According to the context the called are persons toward whom God has omitted no effort, as regards their being invited, with earnest and urgent pleading, to the kingdom of God. But God has expended His efforts upon them in vain. The great majority of them do not obey the call. They are not translated from the world to the Church; they remain *extra ecclesiam*. In this passage of Holy Writ "call" and "conversion" are not identical in meaning. The call, in this instance, is a person's *invitation* to the kingdom of God, without including his conversion. The same meaning appears in two more passages, Matt. 20, 16; Luke 14, 24.

Hence there is Scriptural warrant for using the term "call" *in distinction from "conversion."* Concerning this calling, however, which is not identical with, but must be distinguished from, conversion, two sorts of persons teach error, *viz.,* Calvinists and synergists. According to Calvinism the calling which is not identical with conversion is no call *unto the kingdom of God*, but a mere pretense of calling. Calvin would determine the character of the call by reference to the *result*. This argument constantly recurs in his *Institutiones*: Where no conversion follows God had intended no conversion; for no man can resist the will of God. Now, it is a matter of *experience (experientia)* that not all to whom the Word is brought, are converted. Hence it is folly to speak of a call to the kingdom of God in the case of such as do not actually become converted. All passages of Scripture which teach universal grace he nullifies by a reference to the *ineffectiveness* of the call in the case of many who hear the Word. *Experientia docet*—says Calvin—*ita velle resipiscere quos ad se invitat ut non tangat omnium corda. Experience* teaches that God desires the repentance of some that He calls *in such manner* that He *does not touch the hearts of all.*[153] This exactly is the argument of Charles Hodge, the American dogmatician of Calvinism: "We must assume that the *result* is the interpretation of the purposes of God."[154] Over against this it should be maintained: The call is a divine quantity *in itself*, regardless of the *result*. This is most powerfully exhibited Matt. 22. The king's benevolence, evidenced by the gracious terms of his invitation to the supper he has prepared, as well as his anger, enkindled by the contempt with which his invitation is received, demonstrate the intense, divine earnestness of the calling even in the case of the *ineffectual* call. Matt. 22 is in subject-matter a parallel of Is. 5, 4: "What could have been done more to my vineyard that I have not done in it?" and of Matt. 23, 37: "I would have gathered you—and ye would not." Hence it is quite proper to say that all who live under the sound of the Gospel *may* be converted and saved, as was shown in the preceding chapter. Hence, too, our Confession treats of the call which God directs to all hearers of the Word in such terms as these: "this call of God, which is made through the preaching of the Word, we should not regard as being a mere delusion (*non existimemus esse simulatam*

---

[153] *Institutiones*, III, 24, 15.

[154] *Systematic Theology*, II, 323.

TWO CONCEPTS OF CALLING

et fucatam vocationem), but know that God thereby *reveals His will*, that He would *work* by His Word, in those called in such manner that they might become enlightened, converted, and saved. For the Word by which we are called is 'a ministration of the Spirit,' giving the Spirit, or by means of which the Spirit is given, 2 Cor. 3, and 'a power of God unto salvation,' Rom. 1. And since the Holy Spirit would, through the Word, be active, strengthen, and give power and ability, it is God's *will* that we should receive and believe the Word and be obedient to it."[155] Also the calling which remains ineffectual has behind it the gracious workings of divine omnipotence and the omnipotent workings of divine grace. There are *motus inevitabiles.* Our Confession says of the called who do *not* come: *Veritati AGNITAE perseverantes repugnant,* they offer constant resistance to the truth *which they have recognized.*"[156] The reason why men *are able to resist* the call: Come unto me, all ye that labor and are heavy laden, and I will give you rest,"[157] while they cannot resist the call of doom which summons them before the judgement-seat of Christ,[158] is, because in His call of grace in time God works through means, while on Judgement Day He operates in glory unveiled, (ἐν τῃ δόξῃ αὐτοῦ). Not only in the latter, but in the former instance as well, the operative power is a divine and omnipotent power. "We *believe* according to the working of His mighty power which He wrought in Christ when He raised Him from the dead."[159] But the operations of God through means have the property of being resistible. God working without means, in majesty unveiled, cannot be resisted, as is evident from Matt. 25, 31 sqq., and as is shown at length by Luther in *De Servo Arbitrio.*[160] To say that "the *result* is the interpretation of the purposes of God" is the smart talk of a would-be wise person.

However, also the *synergists* teach error regarding the call as distinguished

---

[155] Mueller, p. 710, § 29. Jacobs, p. 654.

[156] Mueller, p. 603, § 60. Jacobs, p.564.

[157] Matt. 11, 28.

[158] Matt. 25, 31. 32.

[159] Eph. 1, 19. 20.

[160] *Opp. v. a.* VII, 221 sq. St. L. Ed. XVIII, 1794.

from conversion. They distinguish between being called and being converted in such a way as to assert that a *stimulating* effect results from the call. Through this stimulating effect the good *natural* energies dormant in man are roused, and by means of these man is now able to use rightly the powers which grace offers to him. The presumption is that *previous* to conversion a free will in favor of that which is spiritually good, or a freedom of choice in favor of the Gospel, is established through the call. This notion has been expressed thus by the *Lutheran Standard*: "Certainly, where no grace is offered, no consent can be given. But to him who hears the Gospel this grace is offered, *and he may accept and surrender if he will,* or he may resist if he will."[161] Dr. Schmidt, too, expressly taught a *freedom of choice* before conversion.[162] Not all synergists employ such *terms* as Freedom of choice and Neutrality before conversion. But it is a characteristic feature of synergism or Semi-Pelagianism in every form, to attribute to man, before his conversion, powers quickened by the *stimulating (excitans)* effect of the call, which renders man able to dispose himself for conversion, decide for conversion, conduct himself rightly for conversion, cease his willful resistance. Against this conception of the call, as distinguished from conversion, the same general argument must be urged which we presented in the chapter on "Preparation for Conversion," against the notion that *man* prepares for his conversion, and in the chapter on the "Possibility of Conversion," against a *subjective* ability before conversion and in conversion. It positively must be maintained that, if we *distinguish* the call from conversion in the sense that conversion is *subsequent to* the call, then a great deal may come to pass *outwardly* affecting man, but *within* no change has during the call been wrought in man, *i.e.,* there is not yet a spark of spiritual life in man, his will remains unchanged in its attitude of enmity against God. Not until faith is kindled in a person, or he is converted, does spiritual life enter into him, or is his will changed. The call, as distinguished from conversion, is

---

[161] *Lutheran Standard, August 19, 1882.*

[162] *Lutheran Standard,* August 19, 1882. Cp. also Dr. Schmidt in *Luth. Kirchenzeitung*, 26, 15: "Since God will...force no one to be saved, every one retains this choice or freedom" ("either to obey the call of grace by virtue of preparatory and effectively operating grace, or to refuse the same by virtue of self-chosen and willful wickedness and contempt").

the laying siege to a fortress determined upon defense. All impressions upon the fortress come merely from without. An aberration, *in defectu* from the Scriptural doctrine of original depravity must be charged against all who, in consequence of the call as distinguished from conversion, attribute to man a *subjective* ability towards the consummation of his conversion, either by his performing aught that is good or by his omitting evil. *Natural* man is thus credited with a good stock within, an ability to do that which is spiritually good, dormant in man and only roused by the call.[163] Synergism in every form is reducible to Semi-Pelagianism; it makes conversion and salvation dependent on man's ability, and since man possesses no ability in this matter, synergism does all it can to render conversion and the attainment of salvation altogether impossible. God be praised that what men practice is, in many cases, better than the positions which they hold *inter disputandum*!

---

[163] Chemnitz says in regard to this "toying" with the concept "call": *Porro et hoc observandum: sicut olim Pelagius insidias struxit ex verbo adjuvandi,* ita Pontificii in libro *Interim* ludunt vocabulo excitandi: sicut homo excitatur ex somno, ita voluntatem habentem facultatem operandi in spiritualibus tantum quasi cessantem et torpentem somnolentamque excitari. Sed hic ludus et sophisticus et Pelagianus est. Scriptura enim illud: ‚Surge qui dormis' ita interpretatur: ‚Suscitare a *mortuis*', Eph. 5, 14. (*De Lib. Arbitrio*, p. m. 478.)

13

Fellowship of Faith and Church

XIII. Fellowship of Faith and Church-Fellowship with Such As Occupy the Position of Gerhard.

Fellowship of faith and church-fellowship with those who hold Gerhard's position does not cause the slightest difficulty. Such is the clear verdict of experience. Before the doctrine of Predestination was made the subject of public controversy, there were people in the Missouri Synod who held the position of Gerhard. In 1855, Dr. Sihler published in *Lehre und Wehre* a series of 19 Theses on Predestination in which, alongside of the greatest emphasis on "By-grace-alone," he manages to find a place for "In view of faith" in the doctrine of Election.[164] When the controversy on Election commenced and the necessity of treating this doctrine thoroughly on the basis of Scripture and the Confessions became apparent, Dr. Sihler very soon perceived that the intrusion of "foreseen faith" into Election agrees neither with the Scriptures nor with our Confessions. Accordingly, he corrected his theses of 1855 through a public statement which appeared in

---

[164] *L.u.W.* 1855, pp. 234 sq.

Lehre und Wehre in the year 1881.[165] Dr. Sihler's statement is very interesting and instructive. It reads as follows: "It may or may not be known that, with the knowledge and consent of Prof. Craemer, then my colleague at the theological seminary in this city, I contributed, some twenty-five years ago, 19 Theses on Election, to the first volume of *Lehre und Wehre*, which were accepted by the editors...As is well known, this doctrine had not then been controverted, and the experience of all men will bear me out in saying that in such a case no such clear and precise expressions are used, even in the domain of theology, as become necessary when some doctrine has become controverted, and when error has crept in. Now, therefore, since in the very first thesis 'persevering faith foreseen by God' of the elect was given a place in the definition of predestination, I hereby renounce that part of the definition. True, even at that time my way of viewing the matter was, that faith does not determine and condition God's election of the individual—for Thesis 10 says expressly: 'Foreseen faith is not the cause of election, since we are chosen not by reason of our faith, but for Christ's sake' (cf. Thesis 4). But for this very reason the conclusion of Thesis 1 was incorrect and apt to lead to misunderstandings; for it is self-evident, and hence unnecessary to say, that, since in God nothing occurs in succession, but everything is simultaneous, He has according to His omniscience foreseen from everlasting those whom He has from everlasting chosen in Christ by a free act of His gracious will unto eternal salvation and glory, and whom in time He gives through the Gospel faith as well as perseverance in faith. Hence I likewise accept the doctrine of our Scriptural Confession, that solely the free, unmerited, and undeserved grace and mercy of God and the perfect and most holy merits of Christ are the only ground and cause of election." Like Dr. Sihler, a number of other pastors of the Missouri Synod, before the controversy was started, joined the *sola gratia* with foreseen faith. Neither in their case did the attainment of perfect unity in the doctrine of Scripture and the Confessions cause any special trouble. After the general pastoral conference which met at Chicago in 1880, almost universal agreement also in terms was established within the Synod.

---

[165] *L. u. W.* 1881, p. 58.

Whoever really holds fast to the grace of God in Christ and rejects every cause of conversion and salvation in man, and, hence, really holds faith to be *donum Dei*, no longer has any interest in *intuitu fidei* when the correct doctrine of Predestination is exhibited to him from Scripture and the Confessions. For this reason we maintained during the predestination controversy that also Gerhard and the rest of the old theologians would have dispensed with the *intuitu fidei* over against *us*, that is to say, if they had had to deal, not with Calvinists, but with *us* in the matter of predestination. Objection was raised that we could impossibly gauge the possible actions of Gerhard, since Gerhard is dead these two hundred years and more. And this we had to admit. But it were unfair to assume less spiritual knowledge in Dr. Gerhard of Jena than in Dr. Sihler of Fort Wayne. Hence there is no cause for anxiety in the movements toward union now inaugurated. Persons who really occupy the position of Gerhard and Pontoppidan, to speak concretely, persons who really are united on *sola gratia*, and on the rejection of the "dissimilar," *i.e.*, *good* conduct of man, as a means of explaining why some are converted and others not, and who really believe that faith is a *free gift of divine grace* for Christ's sake, will by an inner necessity slough off the *intuitu fidei* husk, to wit, foreseen faith, as a norm of election. This may require varying lengths of time in the case of individuals. It would have been the height of folly had we broken off brotherly relations in 1880 with those who stood like Gerhard. We did what must be approved by every one: we treated the difference with copious reference to the testimony of Scripture and the Confessions, and in this manner attained perfect unity *in rebus et phrasibus*, as is proper in the Christian Church.

The objection might here be made that during the controversy on Predestination we did not convince all, that some left us and adhered to *inutitu fidei*. That is true. But the reason for this was that these people did not hold Gerhard's and Pontoppidan's position. They had not merely identified themselves with the term *intuitu fidei* while otherwise agreeing with those theologians in the doctrine of Conversion, but they were teaching that conversion and salvation depend, as regards their ultimate issue, not on divine grace alone, but on the good conduct of man. As Walther justly insisted time and again, no one can have a grosser *misconception* of the controversy regarding predestination than if he imagines the *intuitu fidei* to have been the main issue in the struggle. The other side took foreknowledge of faith in the sense of foreknowledge of *good human conduct*, and this was admittedly the reason for its adherence to *intuitu fidei*. It has expressly declared the consideration of human conduct to have been the "cardinal point" (*Kernpunkt*) of the entire controversy. While a person holds this position, there is no hope of unity and church-fellowship. But as soon as this position is surrendered and a person returns to the teaching of *sola gratia*, there is, judging from the Missouri Synod's experience, the best hope of unity.

As regards the union movement among the Norwegian Lutherans, perfect unity may be gained simply by continuing negotiations a little farther on the basis of Thesis 5 and Theses 2 and 3. Thesis 5 records an agreement to *reject* every consideration of good human conduct in conversion and predestination, no matter whether good conduct is ascribed to natural or presumably imparted powers. Whoever has accepted this thesis, will, upon due reflection, no longer have any interest in maintaining *intuitu fidei*, or the foreknowledge of faith. Again, in Theses 2 and 3 an agreement has been reached that the form of doctrine according to which faith is an *antecedent* of eternal election, *i.e.,* the form of doctrine characterized by the term *intuitu fidei*, or foreseen faith, is not the doctrine of *Scripture* and the *Lutheran Confession*, but is peculiar only to a number of theologians. All who have accepted this are surely, upon due reflection, ready to surrender the *coordination* of the second form with the Scriptural and confessional form of doctrine. Hence all that is required now is a continuation of courteous and patient negotiations. Then surely all parties concerned will take their position on the "form of doctrine" which is found in Scripture and the Lutheran Confessions.

Two extremes should be guarded against in this matter. The one extreme would consist in an utter refusal to take up negotiations with those who, so far as we can see, are honest in their confession of *sola gratia*, or if we should impatiently break off these negotiations too soon. True, after the American Lutheran Church has discussed the Scriptural and confessional doctrine of

Predestination for more than thirty years, every pastor now *ought to* know what to think of *intuitu fidei* by the rule of Scripture and the Confessions. But we must not forget that not all have taken part in the controversy. If people now hold the view which Dr. Sihler held in 1855, and which was held by many pastors of the Missouri Synod and the Synodical Conference prior to the Pastoral Conference at Chicago, we shall do precisely what we did in the eighties and later. We enter into negotiations with them, and we can see no reason to doubt that the outcome will be a gratifying one. Note well: We always have in mind persons who hold, alongside of *intuitu fidei*, the *sola gratia* and the correct doctrine of the means of grace. While they are still conferring with us in reference to the "theological" employment of the "second form of doctrine," they even now *practice* the "first form" when they think of their own election. For when they think of their own election, they do not think of the inscrutable foreknowing of God, but of their redemption, calling, conversion, justification, and preservation, and hence recognize in the Gospel and the promises of grace their election. We would urge, once more, that, owing to the inscrutability of divine prescience, it is simply impossible to make practical use of the "second form." The old theologians, too, Gerhard, Pontoppidan, and Scriver among them, have never had any practical use for the "second form," but left it on their study-table, where it had originated. That is what is being done in our time. Although, according to the phraseology of Thesis 1 of the Norwegian Articles of Agreement, the "second form of doctrine" has been accepted unanimously and without reservation together with the "first form," still the Norwegian Lutherans will, as little as the German and English, ever make use of it. Because they are even now, as a matter of fact, in harmony with the representatives of the "first form," it would be wrong to despair, impatiently, of the success of the negotiations.

The other extreme would consist in exalting a weakness in knowledge *quasi* to the dignity of a doctrinal norm. If it is certain, on the one hand, that weaknesses in knowledge must be treated in patience and charity, and thus remedied, it is no less certain that they should not be made part of a confessional statement, nor receive the sanction of the Church.

14

Which Side Changed Its Position?

XIV. Which Side Has Changed Its Position?

In one respect this is a *delicate* question. A party-spirit, inimical to the acknowledgement of the truth, is easily roused by a discussion of this question. But a discussion of this kind cannot, after all, be avoided. As a matter of fact, each party has, during the past thirty years and to the present day, maintained that the other has changed its position, and the Norwegian Lutherans had barely accepted the Madison Agreement when the question arose among them which side had shifted its position. United Church voices were heard insisting that the Norwegian Synod's position had undergone a change. And the districts of the Norwegian Synod accepted the Articles of Agreement with the understanding that the leaders of the United Church have surrendered their former tenet, *viz.*, that conversion and salvation do not depend only on divine grace, but also on human conduct. Who, then, has changed his position?

We would not limit our discussion of this point to the Norwegian Lutherans, but would take into consideration also the other Synods which were involved in the controversy. Our endeavor is to treat all fairly. We cannot at this juncture help mentioning by name individuals who were spokesmen of their church-bodies,—Dr. Walther, Dr. Schmidt, Dr. Stellhorn, and others. As to Dr. Walther, it should be said that he always rejected *intuitu fidei*. We have found no utterances of his which would prove the opposite. However, *Kirkentidende* recently quoted expressions of Walther made in 1863 and 1872, to the following intent: "There is a great difference between saying: 'God has chosen those *of whom* He foresaw that they would believe and remain in the faith,' and saying: 'God has chosen some *because* He foresaw that they would believe and remain in the faith, or *because* of their faith.' The former is quite correct, according to Rom. 8, 29; the latter is Pelagianistic."[166] The opinion that in Rom. 8, 29 by προγινώσκειν also a foreseeing of faith is indicated we do not find expressed by Walther in later years. During the controversy,[167] and even previously,[168] he understood προγινώσκειν, Rom. 8, 29, as did Luther, in the sense of "*zuvorversehen*," foreordain, hence, placing it with the synonyms of *erwaehlen*, elect, and in no other sense. Again, Walther's utterances concerning the doctrine of the later dogmaticians extend over so great a length of time and had in view so great a variety of antitheses, that we shall not quarrel with those who would assert that Walther was not always consistent in his judgements. Our own opinion we have stated above, and have given our reasons for the same. But it must not be forgotten that Walther even *previous* to the great controversy wrote: "Our Synod cannot and will not adopt the doctrinal form of our seventeenth and eighteenth century dogmaticians as its own,"[169] and adjudged the terminology of the seventeenth century dogmaticians as, strictly speaking, given umbrage to "an error" which "the theologians themselves execrate,"[170] and for this reason held that we are on the safe side "if we entirely refrain from using the *new* terminology of the seventeenth century dogmaticians and return to the simplicity of

---

[166] *L. u. W.* 1863, p. 300; 1872, p. 132. The same thought might, by some, be found in Dr. Stoeckhardt's utterance at the Chicago Conference: "Prescience does not precede predestination, but coincides with it in one act." (Minutes, p. 86.) But the minutes appear to be defective in this passage.

[167] *L. u. W.* 1880, pp. 135 sqq.

[168] Lectures, 1874.

[169] *L. u. W.* 1872, p. 132.

[170] *L. c.*, p. 139.

the Formula of Concord, which waives every attempt to solve the mystery that here presents itself."[171] So far as Walther's *real position* in the article of Predestination is concerned, no change of attitude can be asserted. This is our firm conviction based on Walther's *very first* detailed utterance concerning the doctrine of Predestination, in his article against Licentiate Krummacher in the year 1863,[172] which so clearly and powerfully states the *limits* within which the correct thoughts concerning eternal election may move, and within which they must be confined, that there is no room left for a real change of doctrinal position thereafter. Walther in this article discusses at length the synergistic as well as the Calvinistic solution of the mystery in Election, and then says in conclusion: "Since the Word of God contains both statements, that God has from everlasting chosen the elect according to the good pleasure of His will to commend His glorious grace, and that the damned are rejected by reason of their own sin and guilt, while the Lord desires the salvation of all, therefore the Formula of Concord believes, teaches, and confesses *both* facts; it does not, like Calvin, endeavor to *bridge* with human *reason* the yawning chasm of this inexplicable mystery, permits both truths to stand, and humbly adores the inscrutable wisdom of God, awaiting the solution of this seeming contradiction in the life eternal."[173] This was Walther's position in the doctrine of Predestination *before* this doctrine became a subject of controversy in the American Lutheran Church. There can evidently be no shifting of doctrinal conviction with one who has taken this position, even if, in the course of time, he might give utterance to variant opinions regarding this or the other theologian, or come short in the understanding of this or the other text of Scripture. We do not hesitate to say that we consider any person orthodox in the article of Predestination who speaks as Walther did in 1863. It may serve the cause of unity, under present circumstances, if we reprint part of this statement by Dr. Walther, *which preceded all public controversy*. Walther wrote in 1863: "The last test whether a presentation of

---

[171] *L. u. W. 1872, p. 140.*

[172] *L. u. W. 1863, p. 257.*

[173] *L. c., p. 298 sq.*

Gospel doctrine contain Pelagian or Semi-Pelagian leaven is to be found in the presentation of the doctrine of Election. Unfortunately, it has been shown by experience that many theologians in their presentation of doctrine avoid and luckily escape Pelagian error only until they begin to treat the doctrine of Election or Predestination. Too often it has at this point become evident that even among those who imagine themselves able to subscribe, word for word, to the confession of the Formula of Concord concerning original sin and free will there are such as have by no means been cured of all Pelagian views. I refer to all those who believe and teach that as the stiff-necked unbelief of many, foreseen by God, is the cause which prompted God from eternity to decree their rejection and damnation, even so the persevering faith of a number of others, foreseen by God, is the cause which prompted God from everlasting to ordain them unto eternal life. Whoever teaches thus evidently represents persevering faith not as a pure gift of divine grace, but as a performance of man and as the external prompting cause which induced the Lord to prefer a number of persons before others and ordain them to salvation. For if faith is a gift of God's free grace, then this faith could not have prompted God to predestinate a person. Faith, in a way, becomes a merit of man, election ceases to be an election of free grace, but is founded on human merit and the moral superiority of one over another, and the ultimate reason for man's salvation is placed, not in the eternal free mercies of God in Christ, but in man himself, his willing, his accepting, his assent, his faithfulness, and perseverance, in a word, it is transferred from the hands of God into the hands of man. If this were the doctrine of the Formula of Concord and of Lutheran theologians faithfully adhering to this Confession, then, indeed, Licentiate Krummacher were justified in charging our Church with being 'infected with a Roman Catholic Semi-Pelagianism,' in spite of its correct stand on the doctrines of original sin and free will. But praise and thanks be to God forever, our glorious final Confession stands also this test. Our precious Formula of Concord has not permitted itself to be crowded from Calvinistic determinism, like some later theologians of our Church, to the opposite extreme of Semi-Pelagianism, even in its subtlest form. For, while it protests against the Calvinistic assertion that God, according to His absolute will, did not desire to save the greater part of the race, but ordained them from eternity unto sin and perdition, hence does not earnestly call them, and that God, accordingly, is the cause of sin and perdition, our Confession, at the same time, is careful not to assert that the cause of the foreordination and salvation of the elect is their better conduct, their constant faith, or taught in them, but asserts that the cause is solely and purely the free grace of God and His mercies in Christ. The Calvinists draw the conclusion: If God has ordained out of free grace a number of persons unto eternal life, if He alone does everything to convert them, to preserve them in the faith, and finally to glorify them, without their contributing the least, then, of course, since all men are by nature equally depraved, the cause must lie in God alone why the others do not become believers, or are not preserved in the faith, and are not finally saved, but damned; the reason must be that He converts and preserves the former through an irresistible operation of grace, while He passes by the latter with His grace, and leaves them in their corruption, because He does not desire their salvation, but has from everlasting decreed and in time created them unto sin, death, and damnation, for the glory of His justice. And it is true, unenlightened reason, which refuses to abide by the Word, cannot but think thus. Reason, ignoring Scripture and following its own thoughts, must draw this conclusion. Not so our precious Formula of Concord, and with it the whole orthodox Lutheran Church. Our Confession does not draw this conclusion. It maintains: That men are saved has its cause solely in the free grace of God; and that men are lost has its cause solely in the sin and guilt of man. It perceives well enough that reason cannot harmonize these facts; it perceives, too, that, according to our reason, if men are lost only by reason of their sin, then the others are saved by reason of their being so much better; or, if men are saved only by free grace, then the others must be lost because of some deficiency in the gracious will of God. But since the Word of God contains both statements, that God has from everlasting chosen the elect according to the good pleasure of His will to commend His glorious grace, and that the damned are rejected by reason of their own sin and guilt, while the Lord desires the salvation of all, therefore the Formula of Concord believes, teaches, and confesses both; *it does not attempt, like Calvin, to bridge with human reason the yawning chasm of this inscrutable mystery*; it permits both utterances to stand, and humbly adores the unsearchable wisdom of God, awaiting the solution of this seeming contradiction in the life eternal."

Since 1881 much has been said on the other side about "New Missouri" and about a "new departure" of Walther and the Missouri Synod. Such opinions are explained, not for the real facts as they are before us, but from subjective state of mind so readily produced by controversy.

On the other hand, we cannot possibly perceive how Dr. Schmidt, Dr. Stellhorn, and the Ohio Synod can square their later with their former position. Leaving out of account all minor matters, such as the interpretation of historical facts, etc., let us just consider the main issue, the recognition of the mystery in Election, under rejection of the synergistic as well as the Calvinistic solution. Since 1881, Dr. Schmidt, Dr. Stellhorn, Dr. Loy, and the Ohio Synod have taught that the converting and saving grace of God is determined by man's good conduct; that hereby is *explained* why some are converted and saved, others not; and that to speak of an inscrutable mystery in this connection would be Calvinism. Now we cannot but believe that *previous* to the controversy, in 1874, Dr. Schmidt in express terms acknowledged this mystery and rejected the Iowaan solution, which would interpolate human conduct. The words have been quoted once before: "Our earnest opposition of the theory of self-determination exhibited and defended by Prof. G. Fritschel in Brobst's *Monatshefte*, should astonish no one, as this doctrine ultimately transfers the miraculous work of conversion from the hand of God into the hand of man, and thus divests it of its real mystery. To render less profound the impenetrable mystery of Conversion and Election, by means of rationalizing speculation, here as with all mysteries of God, amounts to no more nor less than, in effect, demonstrating the mystery as such out of existence. We insist upon retaining the 'mystery of faith' also in this instance 'in order not to be defrauded; for it is not unknown to us what he really has in mind.'"[174] This very position was maintained by the Ohio Synod before the controversy. In the year 1875 the Ohio Synod rejected

---

[174] *L. u. W.* 1874, p. 39.

the psychological mystery consisting in the unfathomable corruption of the human heart, and, as stated in its synodical report, found the mystery to "consist rather in the fact that one is roused, through the divine call of grace, from his sleep of sin, receives the faith, remains therein, and is finally saved, while another also hears the call of God, but does not arise, or if he rises, falls again from the faith, and is finally lost. The cause of our eternal salvation rests entirely in the grace of God; the cause of damnation, in the resistance of man against the operations of divine grace…It will ever remain an unsearchable mystery to human reason why God permits so many to be lost, when He earnestly desires that all should be saved. The Synod finally agreed to substitute for this thesis a paragraph from the Formula of Concord which states this difficult matter with incomparable clearness, and which reads as follows: 'For no injustice is done those who are punished and receive the wages of their sins; but in the rest, to whom God gives and preserves His Word, and thereby enlightens, converts, and preserves men, God commends His pure grace and mercy, without their merit.'" Nor does Der. Stellhorn's statement over against Iowa in 1872, quoted in an earlier chapter, permit of any other interpretation than that of being a rejection of Iowa's "self-decision" and good conduct as a solution of the mystery in Conversion and Predestination. The "psychological" mystery which he *now* confesses is the very one rejected by the Ohio Synod in 1875. One cannot help but posit here a change from the doctrinal position held in former years.

Lastly, how about the *Norwegian synods* which have accepted the Madison Agreement? Which side has changed position? Those members of the United Church which hitherto followed Dr. Schmidt have certainly receded from their former position by the adoption of Thesis 5. Thesis 5 rejects human *"conduct,"* whether proceeding from natural or spiritual powers, as an explanatory cause of conversion, salvation, and predestination, so energetically and persistently demanded by Dr. Schmidt and termed by him the "cardinal point" of the entire matter. Dr. Schmidt's denial of the *certainty of faith* with regard to election and the attainment of final salvation[175] is

---

[175] See footnote 92.

rejected in Thesis 6 d. Dr. Schmidt taught that God alone knows whether a person will die in the faith. Over and against this, Thesis 6 d asserts that also the Christian knows *through faith in the promises of God* that he will obtain the goal of faith. The clearness of presentation might have been enhanced by a brief statement in Thesis 6 d with reference to the *twofold relation* maintained, on the one hand, by the faithful Christian's fear of backsliding (inasmuch as he regards himself and his sinful flesh, 1 Cor. 9, 27)[176], and on the other hand, by his certainty of attaining the blessed end of faith (inasmuch as he regards the grace and promises of God, Rom. 8, 38. 39).[177] Dr. Koren was a master in pointing out this twofold relation. But the substance of the matter has been expressed in this thesis: Uncertainty of salvation for the Christian is rejected, and the certainty of faith is upheld.

As regards the Norwegian Synod, we do not find that Thesis 1, which, taken as it reads, acknowledges the "first" and "second form of doctrine" as of equal authority in the Church, is in harmony with the Synod's former position. True, the Norwegian Synod has ever declared its unwillingness to reject the "second form" as false doctrine so long as it is not made a vehicle for "introducing a difference in man, as if persons who are converted and saved were somewhat better, be it ever so little, than the rest," but permits faith to be simply a gift of divine grace. At the same time, as stated above, the Norwegian Synod declared that the "second form" is "an attempt at finding a solution; an attempt to clear up a great difficulty, to render comprehensible and reasonable what in our opinion must be left unsolved," and, "The first form is very inconvenient for Semi-Pelagians and synergists. Behind the second form they are able to hide, not behind the first."[178] In accordance with this characterization of the "second form," Thesis 1 ought not to read: "The Synod and United Church committees on union acknowledge unanimously and *without reservation* the doctrine of Predestination which is stated in the

---

[176] "But I keep under my body, and bring it into subjection, lest that by any means, when I have preached to others, I myself should be a castaway."

[177] "I am persuaded that neither death, nor life," etc.

[178] Dr. Stub in *L. u. W.* 1881, pp. 473. 472.

Eleventh Article of the Formula of Concord (the so-called 'first form of the doctrine') and in Pontoppidan's Explanation ('*Sandhed til Gudfrygtighed*'), Qu. 548 (the so-called 'second form of the doctrine')." Nor is it in accord with the former practice of treating the doctrinal difference when Thesis 4 leaves it undecided whether Calvinistic terms and words had been ascribed justly or unjustly to the Norwegian Synod, and synergistic terms and words to Dr. Schmidt. That the expression, "man's sense of responsibility in respect of the acceptance or rejection of God's grace," should be amended so as to correspond to Thesis 5, we have mentioned elsewhere. So much on the question, "Who has changed his position?"

Before we close, we beg leave to assure the reader once more that in our discussion we have had no intention of offending any one personally. We would serve the cause of union in the truth of our glorious Lutheran Confession. *Would that the entire American Lutheran Church also in its public teaching might occupy the position which all Lutheran Christians, indeed, all Christians on earth, and all theologians, so far as they are Christians, even now occupy in their relation to God.* It is the position stated by Scripture in the words: "There is no difference, for all have sinned and come short of the glory of God, being justified freely by His grace through the redemption that is in Christ Jesus." Away with "dissimilar conduct" as affording *a means of explaining* why some are converted and saved, and others are not! Back, in simplicity of faith, to the Lutheran Confessions which state with utmost clearness: If those who will be saved *compare* themselves with those who will be lost, they must confess that they, too, conducted themselves *ill* and are in *equal guilt*. At the same time they know from the Word of God that those who will be lost will perish not by reason of any deficiency of divine grace, but through their own guilt. Whatever transcends these two truths must remain a mystery during the present life. The Calvinistic solution, by denying or, at least, detracting from *universal* grace, is contrary to Scripture. Likewise is the synergistic solution, by supplementing *grace* with good human conduct, contrary to Scripture. Let it be said once again,—it is but necessary that all concerned confess that with their lips which they already believe in their hearts before God. May the Lord of the Church graciously grant this through the workings of His Spirit.

15

A Few Opinions that Have Been Expressed

XV. A Few Opinions that Have Been Expressed on This Brochure, and on the Union Movement among the Norwegian Lutherans.

(Supplement to the First German Edition.)

A second German edition of this little book has soon been called for. We beg leave to add, in this edition, a chapter in which we shall note a few of the opinions that have been expressed, both on our brochure and on the entire union movement among the Norwegian Lutherans.

The question whether "the different conduct of men" supplies the "ground of explanation" why they are converted and saved, occupies a prominent place throughout our treatise. By way of criticism the suggestion has been made from the other side that a different mode of procedure would have better served the cause of union. It has been proposed that, above all, we enter upon a very exhaustive *historical* discussion of the conception of "Election." We regard this proposal as impractical. In the first place, historical discussions of this kind are not easily understood by the general public in the Church who necessarily are the arbiters in this controversy. We call attention to our introductory remarks in Chap. IX ("The Position of the Old Dogmaticians"). In the second place, with us Lutherans it is not history, but solely the Word of God which settles questions as to what constitutes an article of faith. Finally, we have reached an agreement ere this as to where the real point of difference lies. We have shown by submitting the documentary evidence, especially in Chapters III and V of this book, that both parties have acknowledged the question regarding the "different conduct" of men to be "the cardinal question of this entire controversy." As regards this point, the respective positions of the parties are clearly and sharply demarcated. Our opponents have declared, quite definitely and decidedly, that converting and saving grace is governed by the correct conduct of man, or, what comes to the same thing, that conversion and salvation are dependent, not upon the grace of God alone, but also on the conduct of man, and that the different conduct of men *explains* why some are converted and saved, others not. We, on the other hand, have contended, quite as definitely and decidedly, that whenever those who are saved are *compared* with those who are lost, there is no such thing at all as different conduct. For, as regards the conduct of those who are saved, that, too, is evil in every instance, and these are in the same condemnation with those that are lost. Accordingly, in view of the fact that there is, on the side of God, a universal and serious grace, and that there is, on the side of mankind, universal and total depravity, it will always remain a mystery, never to be solved for us in this present life, why some should be converted and saved rather than others. When studying the cause why men are saved, we never get beyond *sola gratia Dei*; when studying the cause why men are lost, we never pass beyond *sola culpa hominum*.

More than this. All *accusations* which we have raised against one another are based on our divergent belief regarding "the different conduct" of men. The reason why we have charged our opponents with directly teaching synergism and with repudiating *sola graia* is, because they assume, among a part of mankind, a better conduct over and against grace, and because they make this better conduct "the ground of explanation" why these persons are converted and saved. On the other hand, the reason why our opponents have charged us with *indirectly* teaching Calvinism, a twofold will in God as regards the salvation of men, a divine grace which coerces men and operates irresistibly, etc., is, because *we* teach that the aforementioned correct, or better, conduct over and against grace does not exist in any portion of mankind, and, hence, cannot serve as the "ground of explanation" why men are converted and saved. Thus, then, it is quite manifest hat, if this divergence of belief regarding the "different conduct" of men is removed, peace, serene peace, will enter the American Lutheran Church, as far as the doctrines of Conversion and Election are concerned.

For this reason we have been at pains, from the beginning to the end of our book, to keep this question of the "different conduct" of men in the foreground. To restate the matter summarily: we have proved from *Scripture*, especially bt the example of the Pharisee and of the Jewish nation, and also by the warning addressed to the Gentile Christians in Rom. 11, that Christian faith can neither spring into existence nor continue to exist as long as there is a different conduct assumed as the ground of explanation why some men are converted and saved. Furthermore, we have shown that the *Formula of Concord* declares the different conduct of men to be a *non-ens*, that is, a thing that does not exist at all, and that it adds, in express terms, that the conduct of those who are saved is also evil, and that they are in the same condemnation with those who are lost. Finally, we have demonstrated, not only that all Christians throughout the world, but also all the theologians who oppose us, *as far as they are Christians*, occupy, in their conscience, and when they face God, the position of the Formula of Concord. *Because of the facts*, therefore, we cannot concede the point which the Iowa *Kirchenblatt* makes *viz.*, that our presentation of the matter does not treat the real point of difference, and, hence, cannot serve the cause of unifying the Lutheran Church. Because of the facts, we rather are forced to reiterate our former declaration, *viz.*, that, if a real unification is to be accomplished, it must be accomplished at this point which we have kept in the foreground. To state the matter concretely, that part of the Lutheran Church which has hitherto taught that the converting and saving grace of God is governed by the correct, or good, conduct of man, and has in such conduct discovered the ground of explanation for the *discretio personarum*, must surrender that teaching without any reservation whatsoever. If this is not done, all unity between the parties to the controversy is specious.

This has been the reason why, in discussing the Norwegian Articles of Agreement, we insisted that in Thesis 4 the statement regarding "man's sense of responsibility in respect of the acceptance or rejection of God's grace" be amended, because, if this is not done, the notion of man's "good conduct," which is rejected in Thesis 5, may sneak in again at this loophole. Again, we have demonstrated in Chapter IV that, if the leaders of the "Forenede Kirke" wish to make it quite plain and manifest that they have really abandoned the notion of the "correct conduct of man," as a ground of explanation, it will be necessary that they make three statements, in particular, to wit: 1. a statement to the effect that the leaders of the "Forenede Kirke" have unjustly charged the Norwegian Synod with Calvinism, because they based their charge on the fact that the Norwegian Synod was teaching *sola gratia*, in particular, because it rejected the good conduct of men as the ground for explaining why they were converted and saved; 2. a statement to the effect that the leaders of the "Forende Kirke" have hitherto really spoken like synergists. We had said: "Nor should any doubt be expressed in section 4 whether the other party to the controversy had made *synergistic* utterances. If that is synergism which is rejected in Section 5,—and that is indeed synergism,—then the other party has spoken the language of synergism"; 3. a statement to the effect that in future no person shall be charged with holding Calvinistic doctrine or adopting the phraseology of Calvinism because of the fact that he teaches *sola gratia*, and particularly, because he rejects the good conduct of men as the ground for explaining why they are converted, saved, and elected. We had remarked: "This would clear the situation." And we had added this further remark: "If there should be any who are not ready to five this declaration, this would be conclusive evidence that such have not at heart agreed to Section 5" (the rejection of every cause for conversion and salvation sought in man).

Reviewing all that has been said about the formula "election in view of faith" since the first edition of this book was published, we see no reason why we should add anything to what we have said. In the historical excursus (chap. IX) we have furnished the evidence to show that the dogmaticians of the seventeenth century, who use the formula "election in view of faith," while combating at the same time the synergism of Latermann and Musaeus, do not present the same doctrine as the American champions of this formula. We have, however, added distinctly that assent to this *historical* excursus is not required for unity in doctrine. As regards this particular phrase, *intuitu fidei*, we have shown that, *even when there is no synergistic meaning underlying this term,* it must in no wise be given the right of existence within the Christian Church, because, if this is done, the Scripture-principle is certainly violated. All that we have had to declare on this point we have comprised in the following statement: "However, the relatively favorable judgement which we are compelled to pass upon the old dogmaticians as compared with the American representatives of *intuitu fidei* must not induce the American Lutheran Church to concede to *intuitu fidei* equal rights within the Church with the doctrine of Scripture and of the Confessions. There is a difference between excusing a faulty expression in persons who explain it better than the words import, and to concede to the faulty expression equal rights with the correct expression. Inasmuch as the 'second form' verily does contradict Scripture and the Scriptural confession of our Church, neither an individual person nor a number of persons, nor a Synod, nor several Synods, nor the entire Church has authority to sanction its use within the Church." We have also shown that the theory of *intuitu fidei* has never been of any benefit to our Church, but has caused much harm, that it admits of no practical application, but proves a stumbling-block to the Christian whenever he hears or reads the passages of Scripture which treat of election, because this theory changes the statements of Scripture regarding the relation of election to the Christian's state of grace to their very opposite. Accordingly, we insist that the recognition of the so-called "second-form of doctrine" alongside of the first be striken from the Norwegian Articles of Agreement. The term *intuitu fidei* does not admit of being treated in the same manner as the terms "preparation" for conversion and "possibility" of conversion. These conceptions are posited *in direct terms* in statements of Scripture, as appears from a reference to Gal. 3, 24 ("The Law has been our schoolmaster to bring us unto Christ"), Is. 55,

6 ("Seek ye the Lord while He may be found"), etc. Accordingly, the terms "preparation" for conversion and "possibility" of conversion must be retained as correct, and the enemy who seeks shelter behind these terms must be driven from cover. This has been demonstrated in Chapters X and XI. It would be violating the Scripture-principle if we were to surrender the use of statements of Scripture for the reason that enemies misapply them, and claim them as favoring their doctrine. But the conception "election in view of faith" is not posited in scripture, but is *contrary* to Scripture. This conception is in contradiction of all those passages of Scripture which describe the relation which the Christians' faith and entire state of grace hold to their eternal election. Accordingly, the term *intuitu fidei* must not be given protection, but must be abandoned. We may palliate the weakness of those who give to this term a meaning different from what the words import, and we should seek to remedy this weakness by patient teaching, but we dare never go so far as to place this term alongside of the teaching of Scripture, accord it the right of existence in the Church, and defend it.

We have, even in the first edition (pp. 8 ff.), pointed out the *obstacles* in the way of a unification of the Lutheran Church in the doctrines of Conversion and Election. These obstacles have appeared again during the last three months. Instead of accurately analyzing the contents of the Norwegian Articles of Agreement, instead of carefully discriminating between what is true and what is false, or what is regarded as either true or false, and instead of thus entering upon an objective discussion of the matter, reviewers have rested content with indulging general accusations and eulogies expressed with rhetorical fervor. It is a pity that the slogan "For Missouri!" and "For Anti-Missouri!" still proves to be the decisive factor. Thus in the place of objective discussion there comes greater intensification of the party spirit. The Iowa *Kirchenblatt*, without offering any explanation for its action, reiterates the charge that Missouri has formerly taught, and is still teaching, *Calvinism* (two different wills in God as regards men's salvation, one effectual, the other ineffectual), and that this has caused the controversy on Election in America. We have devoted several chapters to the documentary evidence, to show that the German and the Norwegian "Missourians" have been charged with

Calvinism for this sole reason, because they have declined to consider the good conduct of men as the factor of decisive importance in their conversion and election. The Ohio *Kirchenzeitung* thanks God because the majority of the Norwegians have hitherto refused to listen to the presentations of "Missouri," and expresses the hope that in future neither Norwegians nor any one else in America will give ear to "Missouri." At the same time, the *Kirchenzeitung* claims that "the doctrines for which we have contended such a long time over and against Missouri" have now been "accepted" (*anerkannt*) in the Norwegian Articles of Agreement. This claim is outside of the pale of facts. Even when adhering to its doctrinal position over and against Missoiri, the *Kirchenzeitung* from its viewpoint should word and objective review of the "Opgjowe" about as follows "True, in Thesis 5 of the 'Opgjoer' the doctrine of our Ohio Synod, *viz.*, that the converting and saving grace of God is governed by the good conduct of man, has been rejected. But in Thesis 4 there occurs a statement regarding 'man's sense of responsibility in respect of the acceptance or rejection of God's grace.' In this statement we can find a domicile again for man's 'good conduct,' which has been rejected in Thesis 5. Accordingly, we regard the 'Opgjoer' as a document in which our doctrine of man's 'conduct' is denied the right of existence, but it leaves a loophole for this teaching." That would be the start of an objective review of the "Opgjoer" as regards one point. But the claim that the "Opgjoer" presents the doctrine for which Ohio has hitherto contended over and against Missouri, is seen to be the opposite of an objective discussion of the matter.

We beg leave to offer these concluding remarks: It is verily not well advised for the Ohio *Kirchenzeitung* and other church-papers, to sound the warning cry in the American Lutheran Church because of the union movement among the Norwegians: "By no means listen to Missouri!" *For the sake of the matter under discussion* we cordially request both the Norwegian Lutherans and the Lutherans speaking other tongues: "Do head and examine what Missourians have to say!" With all due modesty we would request that along with others also those statements be read and examined which we have made in Chapter VII: "The point of Difference as Stated by the Formula of Concord," and Chapter VIII: "Assent of All Christians to the Presentation of Doctrine Made by the Formula of Concord." Let these chapters be read and examined. Let the reader try to refute them, at least in his own heart. We are fully convinced that no one, as far as he is a Christian, will refuse assent to what has been said in those chapters. Then, why not bring the professions of our lips into consonance with the belief in our hearts, and thus permit peace to enter our dear Lutheran Church?

SOLI DEO GLORIA!